THIEF,
CONVICT,
PIRATE,
WIFE

THIEF, CONVICT, PIRATE, WIFE

*The Many Histories of
Charlotte Badger*

JENNIFER ASHTON

AUCKLAND
UNIVERSITY
PRESS

First published 2022
Auckland University Press
University of Auckland
Private Bag 92019
Auckland 1142
New Zealand
www.aucklanduniversitypress.co.nz

ISBN 978 1 86940 957 9

Published with the assistance of Creative New Zealand

A catalogue record for this book is available from the National Library
of New Zealand

Design by Carolyn Lewis
Cover art by Xoë Hall, 2021
Map design by Tim Nolan/Blackant Mapping Solutions

This book was printed on FSC® certified paper

Printed in China through Asia Pacific Offset Group Ltd

For
J & G

Contents

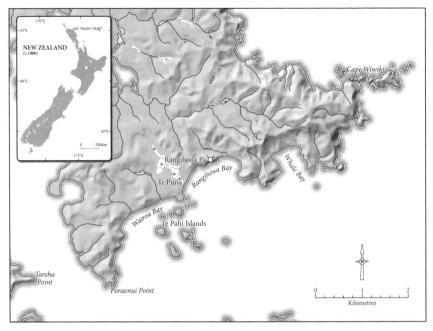

NEW ZEALAND
(c.1806)

170°E
35°S   see main map

40°S

45°S
175°E

0   200km

Cape Wiwiki

Rangihoua Pā

Te Puna   Rangihoua Bay

Wairoa Bay   Whale Bay

Te Pahi Islands

Tareha
Point

Poraenui Point

N

0   1   2
Kilometres

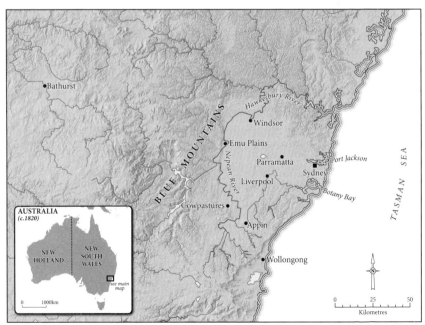

Bathurst

Hawkesbury River

Windsor

B L U E   M O U N T A I N S

Emu Plains

Nepean River   Parramatta   Port Jackson

Liverpool   Sydney

Botany Bay

Cowpastures

T A S M A N   S E A

Appin

AUSTRALIA
(c.1820)

NEW
HOLLAND   NEW
SOUTH
WALES

see main
map

0   1000km

Wollongong

N

0   25   50
Kilometres

Introduction

This is a story of doubt. It is a story of people who left little trace and whose lives are subject to speculation and doubt. There are no writings to pore over; no monuments to gaze at; no perfectly preserved homes to visit. We will never see their faces; we cannot hear the sound of their voices. In other words, they were like most of those who inhabit the past. We catch glimpses of people like them as names in documents recording the major events of their lives. If they lived at a time and in a place where the state was actively engaged in data collection, we might find them coming into contact with the courts, crossing a national border, boarding a ship, or listed as members of a household in a census. But the details of their daily lives remain out of reach. They are the people from whom most of us descend, but for the most part they are mysteries to us.

The woman at the heart of this story, Charlotte Badger, was one such person. Her life, which began at the bottom end of eighteenth-century English society, in many ways remains a mystery, or a series of gaps to be filled in. But she differs from the vast majority of history's inhabitants because her obscurity has not prevented her from playing a role in a nation's history.

Our awareness of Badger owes much to her status as one of the first Pākehā women thought to have resided in New Zealand. Some of

New Zealand's best-known history books, including Michael King's *The Penguin History of New Zealand*, James Belich's *Making Peoples*, Anne Salmond's *Between Worlds* and Barbara Brookes's *A History of New Zealand Women*, have introduced readers to the story of her transportation as a convict to New South Wales and her subsequent escape to the Bay of Islands in 1806. In most of these accounts, though, she is an interesting but unknowable shadowy figure who fleetingly appears before vanishing again. She is a bit of added colour before the story moves on to the main events of (mostly male) missionaries and Pākehā traders and their interaction with Māori in the pre-colonial period.

The regular addition of Badger to the nation's story followed her appearance in the Dictionary of New Zealand Biography (DNZB) in the 1990s. Thanks to the internet, the online DNZB has become a leading means for New Zealanders to learn about her, and her inclusion in recent publications owes much to her entry in the Dictionary. The DNZB tells us that she was baptised at St John's Church, Bromsgrove, Worcestershire, in 1778, the daughter of Thomas and Ann Badger. In 1796 she was convicted of housebreaking at Worcester summer Assizes, and transported to New South Wales four years later, arriving in Sydney on board the convict ship *Earl Cornwallis* in 1801 to serve a seven-year sentence. The entry then says, 'In 1806 she had two years of her sentence to serve, and was an inmate at the old Parramatta Female Factory, where she gave birth to a child. In April she and her friend, Catherine Hagerty, were assigned as servants to a settler in Hobart. In late April 1806 they sailed from Port Jackson on the *Venus* with the child and a group of male convicts.'[1] The *Venus* then became the target of an act of piracy, as members of the crew, abetted by some of the passengers, took the vessel when the master was onshore at Port Dalrymple, now Georgetown, Tasmania. The *Venus* then arrived at the Bay of Islands and dropped off the two women, as well as first mate Benjamin Kelly and another convict named John Lancashire.

Within a year Hagerty was dead and Kelly and Lancashire were gone, leaving Badger as the sole remaining survivor, completely dependent on local Māori. Months later, Badger was offered passage back to Sydney but refused, preferring to stay on and take her chances in her new home. The Dictionary entry concludes by saying that Badger's fate is unknown but quoting one story saying that she might have passed through Tonga a few years later and possibly then gone to America.

The doubt that surrounded her life made her a problematic figure for a publication dedicated to telling the nation's history, but it did not stop her entry in the Dictionary from giving her a new breath of historical life. Nonetheless, historians have been reluctant to take Badger's story much further, and it isn't hard to understand why. We know just enough about her story for it to be enticing but not enough to flesh her out and turn her into a clearly defined historical character. The absence of her own account of her life makes her a difficult figure to get to grips with, and the lack of clarity about her fate leaves an unsatisfying taste in the mouth of biographers looking to write her life story. So, she has remained an ephemeral, fleeting player in the story of modern New Zealand.

My own interest in Badger began with this story that has been told about her. I came across her while researching early contact between Māori and Pākehā in Northland, and specifically a nineteenth-century trader named John Webster in Hokianga. Badger's experience struck me as an early example of the type of cultural interaction that happened in the north of New Zealand in the late eighteenth and early nineteenth centuries, and the challenges inherent in reconstructing such a sketchy life were enticing. While Webster left behind a wealth of first-hand accounts of his life and other useful documents, Badger, who was illiterate, left behind nothing of herself. I began to ask myself, how might such a life be reconstructed?

What's more, when I looked at what I thought I knew of her, she seemed a fascinating figure, and not just because of what she might be able to tell us about the experiences of the shadowy convict runaways who made up a portion of New Zealand's earliest European visitors. Hers was a life lived on a truly global scale. It seemed that examining Badger's movement through time and space could give us a way of understanding what her life, her travels and experience tell us about New Zealand's early relationship with Sydney, the trading nexus between Sydney, New Zealand and Norfolk Island, and the routes across the globe that linked New Zealand to faraway places from the earliest days of Pākehā contact. The pathways of Badger's life could tell us about the Pacific's and, in particular, New Zealand's maritime and trade connections to the rest of the world in the period before permanent Pākehā settlement began in the north in 1814.

As I began searching for Badger in earnest, I was struck by the extent to which she had entered wider culture. The retelling of Badger's story wasn't limited to history books; she turned up in novels, plays, songs, paintings and exhibitions. There was even a restaurant named after her.[2] In most of these versions of her life she was an active player in the taking of the *Venus*, a daring convict pirate on the run from the authorities. In one song, the vocalist takes on the voice of Badger and defiantly proclaims, 'I am not a good person'; in another she and Catherine (Kitty) Hagerty 'stole the *Venus* from under their noses and swore we'd be convicts no more'.[3] In a picture by Lester Hall, she is a dark-haired, thin-waisted, tattooed beauty, the sword behind her back and the skull and cross-bones over her shoulder clearly marking her out as a pirate.[4] Lorae Parry's play *Vagabonds* takes Badger's rambunctiousness to new levels, while also taking a leap of imagination and placing Badger in the middle of the New Zealand Wars of 1863, where she must contend with a group of actors trying to make their way from Waikato back to Auckland.[5] Lisa Reihana, meanwhile, uses Badger's experience in New Zealand as the basis of an exhibition that 'explore[s] the social tension between cultural leadership, spiritual custom and egotistical desire in the face of foreign political challenge in 1800's New Zealand'.[6] Angela Badger's 2002 book *Charlotte Badger: Buccaneer* sticks more closely to the version of Badger's life found in the Dictionary and attempts to put flesh on the bare bones.[7] Written with Charlotte as the first-person narrator, it follows her life from the struggles of childhood and the shock of transportation through to her eventual escape from New Zealand to Tonga.

It would be easy to see Angela Badger's novel, in particular, as simply a way of bridging the gaps of our knowledge of Badger's life, as fiction doing the job that history cannot, and of dramatising the most thrilling episode in Badger's life for its sheer entertainment value. But this proposition does not take into account the other complexities surrounding Badger's story, because once we pick away at even the most basic elements of what we think we know about her, such as her stay in the Female Factory, let alone the more speculative aspects such as the escape to Tonga, we find that at least some of them have been borrowed from fictionalised accounts that filled in the spaces in between sparse evidence and were then repeated as if they were the evidence itself. In the telling and retelling of Badger's story, fiction has become history and history has become fiction, and the result has been the creation of a number of different histories of the same person.

If we look closely at Badger's story, we see that the narratives that have been told about her, and what has come to be seen as her history, have a history of their own. In the almost two hundred years since she was alive, she has appeared and disappeared, been rediscovered and reinterpreted multiple times and in multiple ways, and those reinterpretations have sometimes been the result of feats of imagination. This aggregation, the mixture of fact and fiction, has been happening since at least the late nineteenth century, particularly in relation to the taking of the *Venus*. While the earliest accounts of the piracy barely mention Badger, by the end of the century she was a major protagonist instead of a largely passive observer of events. In the process she has found life after life and has become a person of obscure birth about whom songs have been written and who has featured in historical works, including this one.

The intersection between fiction and history was the subject of the 2017 BBC Reith Lecture series given by novelist Hilary Mantel. In the second lecture in the series, 'Iron Maiden', Mantel made the case for the ability of fiction writers to tell the untold tale: 'They want to give a voice to those who have been silenced. Fiction can do that, because it concentrates on what is not on the record.' She argued that fiction 'can sit alongside the work of historians – not offering an alternative truth, or even a supplementary truth – but offering insight'.[8] She had made this same point in the previous lecture, 'The Day is for the Living': 'I start to practice [sic] my trade at the point where the satisfactions of the official story break down. . . . The historian and the biographer follow a trail of evidence, usually a paper trail. The novelist does that too, and then performs another act – puts the past back into process, into action – frees the people from the archive and lets them run about, ignorant of their fates, with all the mistakes unmade.' On that occasion, though, she had also talked about the contingent nature of history and its relationship to fiction, particularly when it came to the stories that nations tell about themselves: '[W]e reach into the past for foundation myths of our tribe, our nation, and found them on glory, or found them on grievance, but we seldom found them on cold facts.' The myth making extends to individuals, too: 'As soon as we die, we enter into fiction. . . . Once we can no longer speak for ourselves, we are interpreted.'[9]

These observations have relevance for the study of the life of Charlotte Badger. Her appearance in the Dictionary raised her profile as a character in the story of New Zealand, and yet her own story has been constructed and reconstructed over time, and in the process a myth made up partly of elements of fiction and pure imagination has entered the national narrative. But in addition to that, Mantel's comment about the recreation of the life stories of the dead gets to the heart of one of the problems of history-writing: we cannot, despite our best efforts, ever 'know' the whole story of the past; the person who existed and the person about whom we write are always separated by space and time and by both the partialness and the partiality of the evidence they leave as clues for us to follow. Mantel sums up this conundrum, too, noting that 'history is not the past – it is the method we have evolved of organizing our ignorance of the past. It's the record of what's left on the record. . . . It's what's left in the sieve when the centuries have run through it – a few stones, scraps of writing, scraps of cloth.'[10] In Badger's case we barely have the stones, let alone the cloth. And much of what has been left to us comes from record-keeping authorities who encountered her at those points in her life when she transgressed the limits of the law, instead of from her own hand. Yet because of the contacts she made with those authorities we still know enough to judge that she lived an extraordinary life of a truly global reach, even if we cannot see the sweat on her brow or feel the thump of her pulse as she jumped from one obstacle to the next. History cannot deliver her to us whole, but we are not without ways of making sense of her.

To return to the question I first asked myself: how might we go about such a task? To begin with, we can revisit the histories that have been written about her and try to discover where the various building blocks have come from. This approach treats the documented life of Charlotte Badger as a kind of archaeological dig that works away at a pile of layers heaped one on top of the other. This deconstruction risks leaving us with less than we had before, but it can go hand in hand with an act of creation. Once we have identified how her life has been retold over time, we can look at how she helps us understand the historical currents that ran through her life. In doing so, we can expand out the meaning of her life, so that instead of merely being a character in a New Zealand story she becomes a citizen of a wider world. We can take her from the local to the global, from a Worcester courtroom to the outskirts of Sydney, from the English countryside to British imperial trading routes. Then, she ceases just being a minor bit of colour added to the New Zealand story and becomes an active participant in a story that goes beyond New Zealand's shores, but which recognises its role as a destination on a global maritime highway. By changing the point of view from which we view her we can interpret her all over again.

In this way, this study of Badger adds to the series of histories of her life that have been recounted. It offers an interpretation of Badger and the life she led, doing the best it can to base that interpretation on available evidence while acknowledging that that evidence is partial and that history is not simply what happened in the past, it is also an understanding of what happened that we construct for ourselves; it is 'something that happens later'.[11] For this reason, this study doesn't just present a new understanding of Badger, it also tries to explain how and why the various interpretations of her developed, and how they reflected the time in which they were written. It also tries to get to grips with why this woman, of all people, has been given the chance to enjoy a kind of life after death, and why her story has captured the imaginations and attention of later generations.

The version of Badger's life offered here follows the contours laid out elsewhere, including the Dictionary entry, but also differs in significant ways, particularly when it comes to her fate. It was a life that is at once more remarkable, more curious and more mundane than has previously been written. It was characterised by extreme danger as well as domestic tedium; by travel across great distance as well as close regulation. It started in provincial England shaped by the upheaval that industrialisation and an exploding population wrought at the end of the eighteenth century. That upheaval brought with it an increase in the crime rate and a need to find a permanent answer to the problem of what to do with the country's criminals, especially once the American colonies were no longer available as sites of transportation. The choice to relocate the penal colony to the Australian continent came only a few years before Badger's fateful decision to steal from a man of means, which led to her being banished from England and sent to the far side of the world. There, in Sydney, she joined a nascent settlement of convicts, colonial officials, soldiers and free settlers carving out a home that was part prison farm and part Pacific trading station. After five years in New South Wales, she travelled to Van Diemen's Land on board the *Venus* and then found herself headed for the Bay of Islands. In less than a year, though, she was heading back to Sydney on board a government ship from Norfolk Island. At this point her global travelling came to an end, and only a few short years later she became a soldier's wife and spent the rest of her life on the frontier of European settlement, facing out to a continental rather than an oceanic expanse.

In tracing all these aspects of her life, though, we must acknowledge that there will not be concrete answers to many of our questions, and that the doubt that was previously filled by imagination will persist. Instead, we have to accept likelihood rather than certainty as the outer limit of our knowledge – but this likelihood can still be based on the evidence left to us, on the pieces of rock left in the sieve, and it can still reveal plenty about the past. This approach lacks the reassuring conviction that history-writing can give us a clear window into what has come before us, but it allows us to deal with the figures such as Charlotte Badger who make a fleeting appearance in the record and gives us a way forward when we have to accept that we just don't know.

This book tells the story of that life in six chapters, each addressing a different stage, and each looking both at what we can establish about her and the stories that have been told. Chapter 1 looks at Badger's early life in Bromsgrove, Worcestershire. It examines the circumstances around her conviction for housebreaking in 1796 and her subsequent four-year imprisonment in Worcester County Gaol; it puts those experiences in the context of England's treatment of its criminals, especially its female wrongdoers, and asks why Badger avoided the mercy handed out to other women around her, setting her on a path to transportation.

Chapter 2 follows Badger as she is sent to New South Wales. It looks at the voyage itself and the conditions on board, and then examines what is known about her life in Sydney, and considers the treatment meted out to female convicts generally.

The third chapter looks at possibly the most dramatic episode in Badger's life: the piracy of the *Venus*. It asks why she was on board in the first place, introduces the people who joined her on the journey, examines the reasons why those on board joined together to overthrow the captain and take the ship, and looks at the evidence for Badger's involvement in the piracy.

Chapter 4 examines the evidence for Badger living at the Bay of Islands and the story of her life as a cultural emissary. It also looks more widely at the history of the Bay's interaction with Sydney, places it on the Pacific shipping route and studies the traffic that was passing through in order to understand how Badger came to leave New Zealand for Norfolk Island, leading to her eventual return to New South Wales.

The fifth chapter examines the evidence for Badger marrying a soldier in 1811 and spending the remainder of her life on the outskirts of Sydney. It looks at the frontier violence that was happening all around her as she took up residence in Parramatta and contrasts this phase of her life with everything that came before. Finally, it examines, after everything, how far she might have really travelled from her early working-class roots.

The final chapter looks specifically at how the various histories of Badger have changed over time, paying attention to the context in which they were written and considering what they say about the writers and their audience.

The
Accused

There is almost nothing left of Worcester Castle now. Today's visitors who walk the short distance from the banks of the Severn River to the Royal Worcester Museum, or to the ancient cathedral that still acts as the city of Worcester's most distinctive landmark, have no idea of the citadel that once inhabited the riverside site, and probably pay no mind to the curiously named Castle Place. The forgotten castle, demolished in 1830, started life in the eleventh century as one of the fortified buildings erected in the wake of the Norman invasion, and later served the purpose that it would retain for most of its remaining life: that of county gaol. In the 1650s a new brick-and-stone building was constructed inside the grounds. This was home to prisoners until the beginning of the nineteenth century, at which point the crumbling gaol was replaced by a new structure at the north end of town in what became known as Castle Street, in honour of its previous location and because the new prison's design included ornamental turrets.

The old gaol was not only a dominant physical presence; it also acted as one of the sights of the city. On the Sunday that followed the Assizes court sessions held twice a year, prisoners were put on display for the gathered crowds, with visitors paying sixpence to the gaoler as he pointed out those to be executed.[1] Along with the unfortunates awaiting death, in its final years the old gaol held convicted felons to be transported to the penal colony at New South Wales. Some of these prisoners were lucky enough to be pardoned before facing the prospect of deportation; others were held at Worcester temporarily before being sent to the prison hulks, or ships, moored on the south coast that served as human holding pens. Still others stayed for months or even years, enduring summer fevers and living in filth, before being sent directly to a convict transport ship at London. Between 1796 and 1800 this last group included Charlotte Badger.

For Badger, the journey to the castle gaol and the life that lay far beyond its walls began at her home 15 miles away in Bromsgrove. Before she was a prisoner awaiting trial and a convicted felon sentenced to transportation, she was the daughter of Thomas and Ann and the younger sister of Elizabeth Badger. Some accounts of Badger present her as a London pickpocket and a product of that city's slums, but she was baptised in Bromsgrove in 1778, something that can be confirmed by looking at church records.[2] When her baptism took place at St John the Baptist Church, her father's occupation was recorded as 'labourer', marking the family out as belonging to the lowest order of the English working class. It is not possible to know the type of labouring work Thomas Badger did, and for the most part he and his family lived the hidden lives of most of Britain's inhabitants, only coming out of the shadows when official records marked life-altering events or crises. The rest of the time, their daily experience went unrecorded, while simultaneously being shaped by the immense forces bearing down on the small market town that was their home.

Today, Bromsgrove is a tidy if unremarkable service and retail centre which is in danger of being absorbed into Birmingham's sprawl. But it has a long history of its own, stretching back to at least the eleventh century. For most of its life, it has acted as a market town servicing the surrounding countryside and passing travellers, and from the sixteenth century it also became home to a flourishing textile industry. By the time Thomas and Ann Badger were raising their two daughters, the businesses that occupied Bromsgrove's ramshackle streets were based around a range of trades, such as clothier, tanner, weaver, tailor, shoemaker and blacksmith, as well as the provisioning and accommodation of travellers. A visitor to the town in 1814 described it as:

> . . . a large, but dirty place, full of shops, and of manufacturers of nails, needles, and some sheeting and coarse linens. The principal street is long, but straggling; containing some very good houses, whilst many of the more ancient ones are framed of wood, and curiously decorated with black stripes and cross pieces, scallops, flowers, leaves, and other ornaments, of which the glaring contrast of colours produces a most unharmonious effect. . . . The market is on Tuesday; and there are two fairs for linen cloth, cheese, horses, and cattle, on the 24th of June, and 1st of October. . . . The town itself contains about 500 houses, and 3000 inhabitants; but the whole parish consists of 14000 acres, and 3000 of an additional population, of the whole of which, about one half are supported by manufactures.[3]

Of all the trades carried out in Bromsgrove at this time, none was more important than nail-making. By the time Charlotte Badger was born, up to 900 people were involved in producing nails and tacks in numerous small workshops, compared to 140 and 180 workers in the town's two main textile manufacturing trades. Whole families were employed working long hours in this cottage industry, and cramped workshops could be shared by two or three other nail-makers. The brutish conditions were captured in this description taken from the Midland Mining Commission report of 1843:

> The best forges are little brick shops of about 15 feet by 12 feet in which seven or eight individuals constantly work together with no ventilation except the door and two slits, a loop-hole in the wall. The majority of these workplaces are very much smaller and filthy dirty and on looking in upon one of them when the fire is not lighted presents the appearance of a dilapidated coal-hole. In the dirty den there are commonly at work, a man and his wife and daughter, with a boy or girl hired by the year. Sometimes the wife carries on the forge with the aid of the children. The filthiness of the ground, the half-ragged, half-naked, unwashed persons at work, and the hot smoke, ashes, water and clouds of dust are really dreadful.[4]

These filthy industrial workshops, sitting as they did alongside ancient houses, were symptomatic of not just a town but a whole country in a state of upheaval. For better or worse, Charlotte Badger, her family and her neighbours were living through a period of almost unprecedented change that was imprinted on their lives, as well as on the life of the nation itself. Not all parts of Britain were equally affected, and change manifested in different ways in different places. The most obvious impact was in the growth of cities such as Manchester and Leeds built around the burgeoning textile industry, while ports such as Liverpool and Glasgow expanded to send the goods made in the new cities around the world and take in the raw materials like cotton and sugar that were arriving from the slave plantations of the New World. Those who flocked to the urban areas included rural inhabitants who had been driven there by the consolidation of common land into larger, more profitable units. Others came from rural areas or small towns, where they had worked in the cottage industries that would eventually be replaced by the mass production carried out in large factories. Meanwhile, the centre of industrialisation closest to Bromsgrove, Birmingham, became home to a range of industries still built around smaller workshops and manufacturing enterprises.

Although life in the new industrial age remained perilous, and the working lives of most were still conducted in hard and hazardous conditions such as those found inside Bromsgrove's nail-making workshops, there were benefits as well. As the size of towns increased, so, too, did the variety of employment available to those looking for work. In particular, opportunities for some skilled tradesmen increased, while even the prospects of the unskilled also improved, as the range of industrial work expanded in areas such as construction and factory work. The result was that many workers had access to regular wages that allowed them to buy the type of consumer goods that had previously been available only to those at the top of the social ladder, such as sugar and tea from overseas, and domestically produced household items like metal pots and pans.[5]

At the same time, the expanding economy had to make room for an ever-increasing workforce, as the British population rapidly grew. Between 1700 and 1850, the number of people inhabiting the British Isles trebled. A striking feature of this increased population was the number of young people, so that by 1821 39 per cent of Britons were aged under fifteen. These children, with their 'strong backs and nimble fingers', were among those absorbed into the world of work, as a way of providing the labour the growing economy needed and in order to supplement their families' incomes.[6] Although child labour had long been used in Britain as a way of alleviating the distress of poor families, the rapid economic growth that was unleashed by industrialisation saw more children participating in the workforce, and at younger ages, than ever before. Parents who had experienced hardship their whole lives took advantage of the opportunities the industrial age brought to send their children out to work in greater numbers, even as the conditions in which they worked proved punishing. Their decisions were a reflection of their own material circumstances, as children were more likely to be employed if the head of the household was unskilled, or if the family was headed by a solo parent.[7] Children from poor families were also more likely to start working at a very early age, some as young as five or six.

Given their social position and their father's status as a labourer, there is every reason to believe that Charlotte Badger and her sister Elizabeth went to work from a young age. And according to multiple accounts of her life, it was her role as an employee that threw her life into turmoil after she was arrested for stealing four guineas and a Queen Anne's half-crown from the house of Benjamin Wright. A fictionalised telling has Charlotte stealing from Wright while working for him as a housemaid. Other, non-fictionalised accounts also have her working for Wright, as an apprentice. In an article about Badger's life that appeared in a local Bromsgrove magazine, the *Bromsgrove Rousler*, in 2002, Alan Richards wrote that 'when she was 10 years of age she was placed as a parish apprentice to Benjamin Wright of Bromsgrove, probably until she reached the age of 21 years. Benjamin Wright's trade is not known.'[8] Then in an article published in 2005, Ian Duffield repeated Richards's claim about Badger being apprenticed to Wright at the age of 10, and speculated that Wright was a nail-maker who set the young girl to work in the heat of his workshop. In a flight of fancy he added, 'I can almost hear Wright bawling at sixteen-year-old Charlotte, while she hammers like Thor.'[9]

In principle, it is possible that Badger was apprenticed to Wright at the time she stole from him. Apprenticeships provided a way for young people to learn a trade or skill by binding them into the care of a person or family, and ran either for a set period of time (say, seven years) or until the apprentice reached a certain age, most often either twenty-one or twenty-four. What's more, poor children were sent to work as apprentices so that the parish no longer had to support them. It seems unlikely, though, that Duffield's vision of

Badger toiling in the nail workshop was accurate, for more reasons than one. For girls, being an apprentice usually meant learning how to run a household rather than being taught a trade. Between 1700 and around 1820, 301 Bromsgrove girls took up 'housewifery' apprenticeships, while nine took up husbandry, five took up needle making and two were apprenticed as weavers.[10] The odds of Badger being assigned to Wright in order to learn a particular trade are also hampered by the fact that in the will he signed in 1799, Wright is described as a 'gentleman', rather than as some kind of tradesman. It is also clear that he had no wife or children, as he left his worldly goods to his brother and his niece and nephew, and such a man would no doubt have needed someone to run his household.[11] But was Badger the person fulfilling this role?

One problem with answering this question in the affirmative is that neither Wright nor Badger appears in the index of Worcestershire apprentices and masters covering the eighteenth and early nineteenth centuries. Still, it is possible that she was either working in Wright's household other than as an apprentice, or that the index is incomplete. But if she was Wright's domestic employee, with easy access to or even permanent residence in his house, why, in addition to theft, was she charged with housebreaking?[12]

A clue about the nature of their relationship might lie in the fact that when in April 1796 Charlotte Badger broke in and stole his property, Wright wanted to make her face as stern a penalty as possible. In the eighteenth century, victims of crimes conducted more than 80 per cent of criminal prosecutions, rather than the state, and they had discretion over whether to prosecute and, to an extent, over the course of the proceedings. Victims of crime could simply accept the return of the goods taken, and employers often dismissed pilfering workers on the basis that it was 'far easier, far cheaper and, perhaps, less demeaning or embarrassing than a prosecution'.[13] Officials, too, could see to it that the accused faced lesser charges, or made other forms of restitution.

The result was that most petty property offences were settled by negotiation.[14] Even in cases where the offence was serious and where magistrates apparently had little option but to commit the offender to a higher court for trial, they could work in conjunction with prosecutors to discharge evidence. Magistrates might also work as arbitrators who helped the parties come to an informal restorative settlement that allowed the offender to escape the threat of capital punishment that serious crimes attracted. Women, in particular, were likely to benefit from this discretion, at all levels of the justice system, regardless of the seriousness of the charge made against them.[15] Charlotte Badger did not benefit from any of this discretionary decision-making and was sent for trial at the Assizes court, held twice a year in Worcester. The fact that she was shown no leniency suggests that the seriousness of her crime and the evidence against her were damning enough to punish her formally.[16] But Wright's willingness to see her possibly executed for the theft also suggests that they either had no pre-existing relationship to which she could appeal, or any relationship they did have had gone badly wrong. If she had worked for him, the fact that she was charged with breaking into his house in order to steal from him leaves open the possibility that she had been dismissed and was seeking some kind of revenge.

The severity of the treatment she received is compounded by the fact that this theft appears to have been her first offence, or at least the first offence that came before a court. Neither she nor any member of her family can be found facing justice in front of the Quarter Sessions (local county courts below the level of the Assizes), although it is possible that they had been subjected to summary judgment in front of a magistrate for minor offences. There is no evidence, though, to suggest that the Badgers were anything other than a poor but previously law-abiding family, or that Charlotte was in any way a professional thief. This leads us to wonder what caused her to go off the rails.

One obvious possibility is that, as described in Angela Badger's fictionalised account, financial distress was the root cause of Charlotte's fateful and disastrous decision. In this telling, Thomas Badger was a nailer whose work dried up at the same time his elder daughter, Elizabeth, became pregnant to her employer's feckless, debt-ridden footman, Will Gossage. These events combined to throw the family into economic disarray and caused Charlotte to go to work for Benjamin Wright to make ends meet. Wright, however, refused to pay her, and when she saw gold and silver coins lying on a table in front of her, she 'couldn't take [her] eyes off that pile of money. It could buy us so much. We needed flour and tea, and Ma's shoes were beyond mending, Father wanted seeds for the spring and some hooks for the fishing, not to mention a sack of coal which might warm the place up and stop us all coughing.'[17]

There are at least two problems with this version of events, other than the fact that it avoids the charge of housebreaking. Firstly, Thomas Badger was a labourer rather than a nailer; and, secondly, Elizabeth Badger gave birth to her daughter in 1791, five years before Charlotte's crime. In addition, the father of Elizabeth's daughter, Ann, was not Will Gossage but Thomas Haden, a chairmaker. But that does not necessarily mean that the family had not faced serious difficulties. There is a clue in the details of Elizabeth's pregnancy, which came as a matter to be dealt with before the Quarter Sessions. Thomas Haden was called to appear 'to answer the complaint of the Churchwardens and Overseers of the Poor of the Parish of Bromsgrove in the County of Worcester touching his being the Father of a Child or Children begotten on the body of Elizabeth Badger of the same place singlewoman and likely to be born a Bastard or Bastards and become chargeable to the said Parish of Bromsgrove'. Once his and Elizabeth's daughter was born, Thomas Haden was ordered to pay maintenance for her to the churchwardens and was 'hereby ordered into the custody of the Keeper of the House of Correction for the said county of

Worcester until he shall find sureties for the performance of the order'.[18] It is unknown whether Thomas Haden ever accepted financial responsibility for his daughter, but it is clear that without such help Elizabeth and young Ann would become a charge of the parish on the grounds of poverty.

The desire to ascribe Charlotte Badger's crime to desperation is given extra weight by the fact that it took place at a time when Britain was experiencing widespread riots brought on by food shortages and high prices, particularly of wheat and bread. A combination of bad weather, poor harvest and war with France brought the country to the brink of famine in 1795 and 1796, and the resulting protests were the worst in twenty years. Disturbances broke out in locations as far apart as Norwich, Cornwall, Liverpool and Berwick-upon-Tweed, and Worcestershire was among the places that appealed to the Privy Council for emergency supplies of wheat.[19]

Badger's crime also happened at a time when crime rates were increasing across the country. The assumption that dearth and law-breaking were connected is reinforced by the fact that theft was the most common crime, and most thefts were small-scale, leading us to believe that these crimes were simple acts of desperation.[20] The idea that crime was connected to want is also suggested by the fact that the number of people seeking poor relief in England increased hugely at this time, so that 'the cost of poor relief is estimated to have increased five-fold between 1750 and 1803, with the peak increase occurring between 1785 and 1795'.[21] The need to seek relief was often related to life-cycle, as the huge increase in the number of children left parents struggling to cope financially with their new dependants.

But the vast changes taking place in English society had a flow-on to prosecution rates in other ways, too. As Peter King has said, the temptation to steal rose during times of hardship, 'but given the fact that changes in the proportion of victims who chose to prosecute exerted ten, twenty, or even perhaps fifty times more influence on indictment levels than changes in the number of actual thefts, it cannot be assumed that it was the lawbreakers rather than the law users who were mainly responsible for rising indictment rates'.[22] Victims of theft, particularly those who had accumulated wealth in the new industrial age and could now afford to buy the type of consumer goods that demonstrated their affluence and respectability, were reluctant to see their possessions taken from them and were increasingly determined to do something about it.[23]

All this means that a straightforward connection cannot be made between the Badger family's social standing and material condition, Charlotte's decision to steal from Benjamin Wright and her resulting prosecution. She might have been working for Wright either as a pauper child assigned by the parish, or because her parents sent her to work for him to ease the family's financial stress. And it is possible that she stole money from Wright to alleviate the pressure that feeding her young niece had placed on the family, or because her father's income and her own earnings were simply inadequate. But we cannot be sure, and we cannot ignore other known factors, including those relating to Charlotte herself and the specific nature of her crime.

For instance, she does not fit easily into the profile of a typical female offender. Like most women who appeared before the courts, she was young and single.[24] But her crime set her apart in a number of ways. Although there was overlap between the type of items stolen by both men and women, such as food, female thieves were typically charged with stealing very petty items, including clothes and household items, like cutlery and candlesticks. In fact, clothes were the single most common items stolen by women who were subsequently transported, while almost half of them stole either clothes or fabric.[25] Other small items, including jewellery, were often given to pawnbrokers as a way of quickly translating the theft into money.[26] Men tended to be charged with taking more valuable items than women, such as watches. Men were also more likely to break into premises to steal, especially at night.[27] Charlotte's decision to break into Wright's house and take items of considerable value, and in particular money, not only differentiates her from many other female offenders, it also suggests that she was either unusually brazen and opportunistic, extremely desperate, or she was motivated to act against Benjamin Wright for specifically personal reasons. Of course, it is possible that she was motivated by a combination of all three of these factors working together, so that she acted rashly and stole things of particular value to Wright as a way of exacting revenge against a hated employer and alleviating her and her family's distress.

In the end, Badger's fate was most likely sealed by a constellation of factors, all working against her at once. She had broken in and stolen from a man of means who was determined to prosecute her and was willing to take the time and pay the costs involved in seeing her punished. She had done so at a time of anxiety over public disorder in the form of bread riots, and as an untethered youth, about whom society was in a pre-existing and perpetual state of unease.[28] And her status as a single woman acting alone meant she did not benefit from being a mother of dependent children or from being seen as having been corrupted by a male accomplice, two reasons for the judicial discretion from which women were likely to benefit.[29] Together, these factors doomed her to experience something just short of the very worst that the English justice system could mete out.

Three months after she stole from Benjamin Wright that punishment was decided. Once she was committed for trial, she was sent to Worcester and held at the county gaol. Wright and any other witnesses would also have been bound over to appear; any decision on his part not to take the time to travel to Worcester would have seen the whole proceeding fall apart. An indictment would then have been prepared and submitted along with any depositions to a grand jury, whose job it was to assess whether there was enough evidence to send the case to the judge and petty jury at the Assizes hearing. Here, again, discretion could come into play, as the grand jury could return a verdict of 'not found' if they believed that the evidence against an accused person was insufficient. In Badger's case the grand jury offered no such reprieve and the trial went ahead.

When in July 1796 Badger appeared at Worcester summer Assizes charged with housebreaking and theft, she was one of seven prisoners convicted that day, and the only woman in the group. The others came from across Worcestershire and had committed a range of crimes. Joseph Vaughan had stolen three sheep from Thomas Mason; John Jones had stolen four bottles of rum, one bottle of wine and six guineas; Charles Wood had demanded money from Jane Goodman and had broken her skull when she refused to hand it over; Thomas Parry had stolen six ewes and five lambs at Much Marcle; John Jenkins had taken a box containing nearly £18 from the house of Robert Evans in Kidderminster; and William Davis had stolen money from Joseph Marsh. All seven were sentenced to death. It took an agonising four months before the judge's request that they be treated mercifully was agreed to by the Home Secretary, the Duke of Portland. In Charlotte's case, mercy amounted to seven years' transportation to New South Wales.

Not everyone tried at Worcester for similar crimes was spared the executioner's noose. On the wall in the cells underneath Worcester Guildhall, which acted as the site of the Assizes court, is a list of those executed at Worcester from 1800. Most of those who suffered the death penalty had been convicted of forging banknotes, which was viewed as one of the nation's most serious offences. But more mundane crimes could also carry the ultimate punishment. In 1800 two men by the names of Atkins and Watford were executed for sheep stealing, and in 1803 Richard Colledge was hanged for horse theft. Three years later, John Davenport and William Lashford were executed for burglary. In 1798, during Badger's time inside the gaol, four men were executed.

The knowledge that execution was a realistic, if relatively rare, possibility must have added an unbearable tension to an experience that was already designed to overawe the accused. For the prisoners like Badger who came from Worcestershire's smaller towns, even being in the county's main city, probably for the first time, would have been disorientating. When combined with the isolation and discomfort of the castle gaol that acted as their home in the time leading up to their trial, a sense of dread and fear must have settled on even the most resilient soul. On the day of the trial prisoners were transferred to the cells underneath the guildhall, an imposing building described by a contemporary as 'justly esteemed the most elegant and magnificent of the kind in the kingdom'.[30] Built in 1721, it was, along with the cathedral and the gaol, probably the largest structure the prisoners had ever seen. When their turn before the judge arrived, the accused climbed the stairwell that connected the cells to the hearing room above.

The scene that awaited them added to the feeling of intimidation. This effect started with the hearing room itself. On the wall above a blind Justice were the words *Fiat Justitia, ruat Caelum*, Let justice be done though the heavens fall.

Then there was the judge. Assizes judges were often 'the most immediate and accessible representatives of the ruling classes in the provinces, and were perceived as persecutors of the poor and defenders of the interests of the rich and powerful'.[31] This perception was compounded by the fact that the jurors were all property owners whose interests were more likely to align with the aggrieved victim of the crime than the working class who made up the majority of the accused. The centrepiece of the trial, the presentation of evidence, presented another challenge in that it involved a face-to-face confrontation between the accuser and the accused, rather than a back-and-forth between lawyers. The person on trial would be expected to answer for their alleged crimes, sometimes without knowing the exact charges they were faced with in advance, and without being told of the evidence against them. And their ability to offer a defence was hindered by being held in gaol ahead of time. Sometimes trials lasted only a few minutes before the jury huddled in the corner and considered a verdict. The accused had little option but to wait as this small group decided their fate, praying their life would be spared but anticipating the shock of the final judgment.

The culmination of Charlotte Badger's trial with the decision that she would indeed be punished by death seems, to present-day readers, almost bewildering in its harshness, but the horror of being told that you had forfeited your life was a common experience for England's convicted thieves. Between the middle of the seventeenth century and the mid-eighteenth century, in what became known as the Bloody Code, the number of offences that attracted the death penalty rose from around 50 to more than 150. Most of these offences were property-related, and included crimes ranging from horse and cattle theft to highway robbery, arson, forgery, pickpocketing and housebreaking. The authorities' desire to visit severe punishment on property offenders may have reflected their need to maintain control over a growing, urbanised, mobile populace. It has been argued that 'the increasing arsenal of death laws provided the Whig rulers of England with a functional combination of threat, terror and mercy that established their hegemony over the "loose and disorderly" mass of the population'.[32] In reality, mercy usually won out over terror, given that by the early nineteenth century 86 per cent of those found guilty were having their sentences commuted.[33] The reason for this was not entirely altruistic, however, and more likely reflected the ruling class's awareness that it was counterproductive to overuse the ultimate penalty. Evidence also suggests that officials in areas of the country away from London were reluctant to activate the Bloody Code, reflecting the limits of the state's power in these places and the need to balance the punishment of property crime with local conditions.[34] All of this meant that, when Charlotte Badger had a sentence of death passed on her, she was one of the majority who escaped with their life but not with their freedom. And the relief of being spared would ultimately have been tempered by the uncertainty and the enormity of what came next.

After sentencing, she was sent back to Worcester County Gaol at the castle, first to await the outcome of her appeal for clemency, and then, when that was granted, to spend the next four years preparing herself for transportation. It is not known whether she ever saw her family again. At this time in England, gaols weren't seen as places of reform, and even imprisonment wasn't a common form of punishment for serious offences. The exception was the bridewells, or houses of correction, which had been established in the late sixteenth and early seventeenth centuries as places where vagrants, petty offenders or otherwise troublesome people could be set to work. Thomas Haden had been condemned to such a place for failing to support Elizabeth Badger and their newborn child. Gaols were, however, mostly temporary holding places for those awaiting execution or transportation, or for debtors. Badger's extended stay in the castle gaol, therefore, wasn't meant to improve her character, but merely to separate her from society until she could be sent across the sea.

Once there, she joined twenty-seven other convicted felons, including three other women. This relatively small number remained stable over the coming years. In 1802, for example, two years after she left the gaol, it housed twenty-one felons and twelve debtors. Another twenty-three prisoners were being held in the bridewell that took up one end of the castle building.

Despite the fact that the gaol usually accommodated only a small number of people, it still failed to adequately house its inmates and separate different types of prisoner. Male prisoners had access to their own courtyard during the day, but it was shared by 'persons committed for, or adjudged guilty of Misdemeanours, those committed till trial for Felonies, the Convicted Felons, and Transports'. The same applied to the day room and to the sixteen cells where the prisoners slept at night. The cells were prone to overcrowding, with 'the Gaoler having at times been obliged to confine two, three, and some times more Prisoners at night in one cell', despite the fact that they measured only 10 feet by 7 feet in diameter.[35]

As with the men, the female prisoners had their own, smaller yard and a day room, but they were assigned only two sleeping cells, which all classes of prisoner shared. Male and female felons were kept apart. But there was no separate accommodation for children, or even for 'such persons as are intended to be examined on behalf of the Prosecution of any indictment for Felony'. Instead, inmates were left to form what one morally panicked observer called a 'profligate Society; where the most ignorant may be initiated, and the novice ascend to the higher mysteries of infamy and vice'.[36]

If their surroundings endangered the inmates' moral well-being, the diet was likely to have a less ruinous effect on their physical health. Convicted felons were given one pound of bread each day and a quart of oatmeal gruel for breakfast. The dinner menu for the week comprised the following:

> Sunday, half a pound of meat, and one pound of potatoes.
> Monday, two pounds of potatoes.
> Tuesday, a quart of pease soup.
> Wednesday, two pounds of potatoes.
> Thursday, the same as Sunday.
> Friday, two pounds of potatoes.
> Saturday, a quart of pease soup.[37]

While at first sight this seems like an uninspiring offering, it was at least no worse than the diet of a typical labouring family, and the presence of meat on the menu twice a week might even have been an improvement on what some inmates were used to.

There were other benefits as well. Convicts awaiting transportation received an allowance of 2s 6d per week, while other prisoners were able to work at spinning, carding wool, making bags, sacks and gloves, beating hemp, pounding sand, and dressing leather, from which they received a portion of the proceeds as earnings. Prisoners also received coals to use as fuel during cold months.

No such assistance was extended to the debtors held at the gaol, and as a result they suffered the greatest hardship, especially those held in what was called the Common ward. These wretched souls, who had been imprisoned until they had cleared their debts to their creditors, were not fed, were charged for the most basic amenities, such as bedding, and were given no fuel with which to warm themselves or cook, a far cry from the fictional comfort enjoyed by Mr Dorrit.[38] Men and women were confined together, although women who could afford to might pay for a bed in the gaoler's house.[39]

In 1794, twenty-two debtors from the county and city gaols sent a petition to the House of Lords asking for relief:

> That there are at present in this Prison 22 Debtors who have belonging to them 14 wives and 77 children that they are in general without property and from their situations unable to contribute to their own support and are left with their helpless families dependent on precarious charity to preserve them from perishing under the last Extremes of human misery; That all experience proves how little any purpose of Justice is or can be answered in general to Creditors By the confinement of the persons of their Insolvent Debtors who are without any Relief against the personal severity of their Creditors bent on punishing them with all the sufferings of unlimited confinement. That independent of the sufferings and injuries experienced by Debtors in confinement they are themselves the unhappy witnesses of the growing Injuries to the Publick as the unavoidable consequence of Imprisonment for Debt.

Your petitioners therefore most respectfully indulge the
hope that this Right Honourable House may in its wisdom
justice and Humanity be Disposed to make some provision for
the Debtors confined in these gaols and they therefore most
Earnestly implore their Lordships to take their unhappy case
into consideration and to grant them such Relief as Parliament
shall in their Wisdom think Proper.[40]

There is no record of how the Lords responded, but an account of
the gaol in the early nineteenth century leaves little room to doubt
that they received no meaningful relief.

For all prisoners, regardless of their status, life in the gaol was
cramped, dismal and hazardous, and brought the distress of being
separated from their homes and loved ones. Some were ready
to risk further punishment in order to rejoin the outside world,
something made easier by the crumbling state of the gaol, which
literally opened up the possibility of escape. In 1807 a visitor noted,
'There is a crack of some extent in the wall that separates the men's
from the women's ward. The Gaoler has great merit in guarding his
prisoners as the means of escape are easy to an active man.'[41] That
same year, Lord Macdonald arrived at Worcester to oversee the
Assizes only to discover that many of the prisoners due to appear
before him had vanished. In the April before Badger's trial a similar
mass breakout had been attempted, but had failed. One of the five
men involved was John Jenkins, who had appeared at the summer
Assizes with Badger three months later. As a result of his actions
Jenkins found himself 'confined in cells kept from all conversation
with the other prisoners for one week'.[42] The ringleader was chained
up in the 'condemned room'. Another man, John Owens, attempted
escape from the solitary cell he was confined to and was consequently
locked up in the dungeon.

Local magistrates regularly visited the gaol, recording their
impressions of the prisoners themselves and the conditions in which

they were living. Some entries in the visiting book painted the gaol as well run and the inmates as orderly and well behaved. For example, on 3 May 1796, around the time Badger became a prisoner, the magistrate wrote he had '[v]isited the Gaol and found every thing in good order & all prisoners orderly in their behaviour.'[43] But these statements of confidence in a well-run institution were undermined by repeated concerns about the moral and physical well-being of the inmates.

By far the most serious threat to health came from the gaol's dilapidated water supply. Water was supposed to be pumped into the gaol from the Severn River, but during Badger's time there the pipes were simply not up to the task and repeatedly failed. On 3 May 1796, the visiting magistrate's assertion that the gaol was in good order was contradicted by his observation, 'The prison still but indifferently supplied with water.'[44] By July, the heat of summer combined with the lack of water had left the inmates suffering from fever and unable to work. The following month the visiting magistrate wrote that:

> The want of a regular supply of water is of a very serious
> tendency & as the pipes are entirely out of order I wrote a
> letter to the managers or commissioners of the water works
> requesting their immediate attention to the repairs of them.[45]

Less than a year later the situation had deteriorated to the point where the inmates' health was at serious risk:

> *15 Feb 1797*
> Visited the Gaol and found the Prisoners employed in carrying
> water to fill the Bath with intent to let it down the sewers to
> clean them of their filth which is so great that they are stopped
> up and there privys are so full and the stench so great that
> the worst consequences may be expected if a remedy is not
> immediately applied.[46]

22 Feb 1797
All the pumps exhausted in supplying the bath.

  The common sewer or drain which passes thro the Felons
court not having been sufficiently scoured of late, as heretofore
by the discharge of the Bath into it, in consequence of the
failure of water so long complained of in the prison, the
necessaries are become overcharged and the air rendered
thereby very offensive.[47]

The exhausted state of the water supply was never resolved, and in
the end became one of the reasons for condemning the old gaol and
relocating to Salt Lane in 1813.

  The filth that pervaded the gaol ended up taking its toll on the
prisoners' bodies in other ways, too. On 18 February 1797, the
magistrate found 'many of the prisoners very ragged and absolutely in
want of decent clothing'. A year later the visiting book noted many
of the prisoners were 'in a dirty and indecent state as to their clothes'.
The inmates suffering in this way included Charlotte Badger:

  7 July 1797
  Charlotte Badger a female convict under sentence of
  transportation being destitute of clothing we do order that the
  Gaoler provide such things for her as are necessary, also a pair
  of shoes for Mary Justin.[48]

Towards the end of her time in the gaol, she was found to be in
a similar condition, and another new shift dress was immediately
ordered for her.

  Then there were the magistrates' concerns about overcrowding,
which centred particularly on the female inmates. The limited space
afforded to them, when coupled with the fact that all classes of
female prisoner had to associate together, meant that conditions
could quickly become noisome. In 1799 the gaoler recommended

that Badger and some of her fellow prisoners be granted a respite
from their situation:

> *31 January 1799*
> The gaoler having reported to us that there are nine women
> confined in the County Gaol, seven of whom are under
> sentence of transportation and two committed to take
> their trials for house breaking and that there being but two
> women's cells in the said gaol, in consequence of which seven
> of the women are obliged to sleep in the day room which is
> attended with much inconvenience, and the gaoler having
> recommended the following women (being part of the above
> number under sentence of transportation) as being very orderly
> and decent in their behaviour – ordered that Martha Evans,
> Sarah Leland, Charlotte Badger & Sarah Baylis be removed
> for safe custody to the County Bridewell.[49]

The previous year the visiting magistrates had written to the
Duke of Portland asking if some of the female prisoners awaiting
transportation could be moved to the hulks as a way of alleviating
overcrowding. The reply came back saying there was currently no Act
of Parliament that allowed for female convicts to be accommodated
on the hulks, and that the women would have to wait until they
could be sent to New South Wales.[50] As an alternative, the magistrates
turned to freeing the women instead. In the same letter denying
the request to send female convicts to the hulks, two pardons were
granted: one to Mary Justin and the other to Ann Mayfield. By
1798, Justin, who had been sentenced to seven years' transportation,
was sixty-two years old and suffering from rheumatism. Both she
and Mayfield were described as well-behaved and orderly prisoners.
The magistrates also noted that Mayfield, who had been confined
for four years, was 'very industrious: she & her family have a very
good character shewn to us'.[51]

In 1799 a free pardon was also granted to Elizabeth Jones, who had been found guilty of shoplifting. And a year later the visiting book noted, 'His Majesty having granted a free pardon to Sarah Baylis & she being destitute of money ordered that the Gaoler do provide half a guinea to pay her expenses to Birmingham, & that he do charge the same in his bill.'[52] Baylis had been convicted of burglary and had been in the gaol since 1797.

These displays of mercy undermine the view of English gaols as sites of deliberate cruelty, best captured in the somewhat overheated prose of Robert Hughes in his popular work about the convict system, *The Fatal Shore*. Relying on John Howard's report on the state of prisons in England and Wales published in 1777, Hughes described these places as a 'hidden world, of which the respectable and literate knew nothing – its crowding, darkness and scant rations, the cruel indifference of the Bench and the venal favoritism of the wardens, the garnish and chummage and easement fees, the cell floors awash with sewage, the utter lack of medical care, the fatal epidemics. Even the air was unbreathable.'[53]

Worcester County Gaol was indeed a wretched place, injurious to the health of its inmates. Debtors were trapped in a cycle of poverty, while felons had their skin flayed by the whip or were hanged in front of crowds waiting eagerly for them to pass out of the world. Those prisoners locked up with the condemned experienced first-hand Dickens's description of the awful contact with death among the young 'in full health and vigour, in the flower of youth or the prime of life, with all their faculties and perceptions as acute and perfect as your own; but dying, nevertheless'.[54] But Worcester had escaped the worst criticisms that Howard had levelled at other prisons, and the magistrates charged with overseeing it did not show unthinking callousness to the circumstances in which prisoners lived. They took practical steps to address the worst of the conditions, and when overcrowding could not be relieved they were willing to send long-term prisoners back to their homes and families. And they eventually heeded calls to replace the gaol altogether, leading to its closure in 1813. Their decisions reflected the influence that officials had in shaping elements of the criminal justice system and the treatment of prisoners at the local level.

But they also highlight Charlotte Badger's misfortune in not receiving the same kind of mercy as some of her fellow prisoners. When she was sentenced in 1796, she was one of four female felons being held in the old county gaol. By the end, only she and Martha Evans remained, while the other two, Mayfield and Justin, had been freed. This was despite both Badger and Evans being 'very orderly and decent in their behaviour' and having already served the bulk of their seven-year sentences. In fact, even Evans seems to have escaped transportation as her name doesn't appear on any convict shipping list. Instead, when Badger was finally sent for transportation in 1800, she was accompanied by three other women who had been in the gaol for a shorter period of time than her: Sarah Layland, Sarah Hill and Hannah Hall.

It is impossible to know why the magistrates' merciful eye passed over her, particularly given that her crime was similar to those of Mayfield, who had been convicted of housebreaking, and Justin, who had been found guilty of stealing goods and money. But their decision not to grant a pardon meant that, instead of returning to Bromsgrove and picking up the pieces of her old life in the way her fellow female inmates had been allowed to, she was sent away from everything she had known, forever. That decision was simply the latest in a series of choices, starting with her indictment and conviction, that, when taken together, saw her banished from Worcestershire to the other side of the globe.

Her early life had been characterised by the closeness and restriction that came with the limited opportunities afforded to working-class girls in a small market town, followed by four years of captivity and physical confinement. She had escaped death but had watched her life become circumscribed by the inside of prison walls. Now she would be cast out into a world of unimaginable vastness.

The
Convict

Charlotte Badger's first trip beyond the boundaries of Worcestershire came in the summer of 1800 on a bone-shaking journey to London. This was the beginning of an almost year-long voyage to New South Wales, which twelve years earlier had been selected as Britain's new solution to its burgeoning prisoner population. Most likely, she made the journey in a cart packed with other women from county gaols as it rattled along dusty, rutted roads to the capital. Once there the women were joined by men from Newgate and other prisons, and later on by men who had been held in the hulks moored on the south coast. Then, in a pattern that repeated itself over and over during the years of transportation, the convicts were washed and given new clothing before boarding their transport ship, and those whose vessel called at Portsmouth underwent inspection after embarkation to make sure they were healthy. If they failed, their expulsion from Britain would wait for another day.

The voyage that awaited those fit for transport from Britain halfway across the world to the new settlement at Sydney Cove was a trial of endurance, of pitching and heaving on the open ocean in a ship packed with human cargo. In the early years, convicts had to share the limited space on board with provisions for Sydney's inhabitants, making an already tight situation even more cramped. On top of this, life below decks could be dark, airless and dank. As water seeped through cracks in the ship's hull, bunks and bedding became wet, and in heavy seas, when the prisoners were confined below decks, water often swirled all around them. The calm seas of the doldrums could be even worse as the stench of crowded humanity mixed with fetid sea water proved inescapable. Respite came only from stopovers at Rio de Janeiro and Cape Town, where the convicts and crew alike might get their hands on the fresh food they needed to stave off scurvy and other illness.[1]

The horrors that could accompany such a journey had been clear since June 1790 when the Second Fleet limped into Sydney minus a quarter of the roughly one thousand male convicts who had started out. Almost half of those who arrived alive were ill with scurvy or fever, and 40 per cent were dead within eight months. Many had been physically unable to make their own way off the boat or to stand unassisted for the first time on the land to which they had been banished; almost all were covered in lice. The shock reverberated back to England so that no one could be ignorant of what might lie in store during an ill-managed trip. Improvements were made and mortality rates declined from 1800 onwards, but the lives of convicts were still at risk. In 1799 the *Hillsborough* set sail from Langstone Harbour near Portsmouth with around 300 convicts; only 205 survived the trip. The ship had set out during an outbreak of typhus and authorities had ignored calls not to load the passengers.[2]

Badger made her version of this journey the year after the *Hillsborough* on board the *Earl Cornwallis*, a three-decker East Indiaman that had been launched on the Thames in 1783. Over the next seventeen years, it made seven voyages to India and China, calling at the ports Madras and Hong Kong, via places such as St Helena, Madeira and Malacca, and carrying spices, cotton and tea for British consumers. In 1800 it was sold and made its only trip to New South Wales as a convict transport, departing on 18 November that year. The loading of the 295 convicts had started some considerable time before, though. At the beginning of September, the ship moved from London to the Downs anchorage, off the Kent coast at Deal. From there, the fifth mate, Robert Scott, wrote to his mother, 'We have 100 women and 100 men on board at present & will take 100 more men at Portsmouth, they seem all very hearty and contented.'[3] Scott's claim of convict contentment was a triumph of wishful thinking right from the start, but two months later the convicts must have thought they were trapped in a floating purgatory of destiny delayed. By the middle of September, the ship had moved on to Portsmouth, but a month later it was still waiting at Cowes for stormy weather to abate. It took another month before the vessel finally got under way.

The 193 men and 95 women on board were drawn from across England, from Somerset and Devon to Sussex, Kent and Norfolk, and up to Lancaster, Northumberland and York. There was even a lone Scot, a woman from Stirling. Badger was one of six transportees who had been convicted at Worcester Assizes, including Sarah Layland, Sarah Hill and Hannah Hall, with whom she had shared the confines of Worcester County Gaol. They were joined by another woman, Elizabeth Ruck, and a horse thief named Joseph Hodgkins, who had entered the gaol in 1799. Sharing the female quarters with Badger and the other Worcester women were prisoners who had committed the kind of pilfering typical of female convicts. Charlotte Jennings had stolen curtains, pillowcases and sheets from the room she rented in London, while Sarah Trapnell from Somerset and Elizabeth Voller from Southampton had stolen handkerchiefs. Sisters Frances and Philadelphia Pounds had broken into a house in Kent and taken shoes, clothing and food. Unlike

Badger, these housebreakers had been sentenced to life. There were more obviously troublesome cases, too. Elizabeth Hurley was 'a vagrant found at large, feloniously wandering abroad and begging after having been imprisoned as an incorrigible rogue'; similarly, Mary Edwards, another Devon vagrant, had been deemed incorrigible. Martha Anderson, meanwhile, described as 'an idle and disorderly person', was transported for larceny.[4]

As the ship finally made its way down the Solent and out to sea, those prisoners like Badger who had never previously seen the ocean let alone spent time on it must have struggled to gain their sea legs while battling the simultaneous curses of seasickness and homesickness. From the confines of the lower decks they had said goodbye to the homeland they would never see again without any guarantee that they would arrive safely at the other end.

Like other early convict transports the *Earl Cornwallis* dropped down across the Atlantic to Rio de Janeiro and then eastward to Cape Town. From there it was a straight run across the Southern Ocean to Sydney. Once under way the convicts would have settled into some kind of routine, with the women taking on the responsibilities of cooking and attempting to keep both their and the men's quarters clean. Performing these duties allowed the women to fulfil their expected domestic role, although the daily work routine was less structured in the early phase of transportation than it was from about 1817. The move towards a more ordered environment reflected authorities' fears about what the women were getting up to in their spare time, as well as a desire to moderate the more disorderly aspects of their behaviour and to have them adhere to ideas of feminine decency. Recollecting his six voyages to New South Wales in 1827, Peter Cunningham claimed that cohabitation between female convicts and crew had been rife early on,[5] while in her study of female convicts, Joy Damousi also claimed that '[c]onvict women would certainly have had more opportunity to enter into sexual liaisons with the officers and seamen during the earlier transportation phase, when their daily activities were not so rigidly structured.'[6] We can't know how common these relationships were on the *Earl Cornwallis* or if Badger found herself involved in one, but at least one woman, sixteen-year-old Jane Horrell, met her future husband, William Eckford, a free passenger, during the trip. It also seems likely that although for some women sex was a matter of pleasure, for others it was, at best, a matter of practicality. As Babette Smith has said, 'the women were largely at the mercy of the male passengers, officers and crew, even if it was only to exchange sex willingly for extra privileges'.[7]

Women found other ways of dealing with life on board, too. Cunningham recalled, 'They danced several times weekly in the evenings throughout the voyage [and] kept up singing for an hour or two every night before retiring to bed'.[8] In the diary she kept during her voyage to New South Wales on board the *Speedy* in 1799–1800, Anna King, wife of future governor Philip Gidley King, also commented on the all-female convict passengers' liking for dancing: 'The ladies seem all very happy and by way of a treat they had a little dance for about two hours – it was much amusement to us to look at them, some attempted Irish, other Scotch steps and in truth I could scarcely make out any sort of steps.'[9]

At other times they had no option but to hunker down against the violence meted out by the weather. Nothing is known about the first two legs of the *Earl Cornwallis*'s voyage, but according to Scott the final leg was an ordeal by sea and air. He wrote to his mother that during the seven-week trip from the Cape, 'It blew a continual Gale of wind most all the passage, with most tremendous squalls.'[10] Seasickness wasn't the only threat to the passengers' health. When the ship finally arrived at Sydney on 10 June 1801, scurvy was rife and thirty-five convicts were dead from dysentery. Acting Governor King reported to the Transport Commissioners that '[m]any of those landed are extremely weak and feeble.' He also reported that some of the provisions had been ruined by water, suggesting that the ship had leaked, making conditions on board difficult, to say the least. Despite these trials, Badger and her cohort apparently took the suffering in their stride, given that King also reported, 'No complaint has been made of improper treatment during the voyage, and what is very extraordinary no complaint has been made by the agent or master of any very bad behaviour of any of the prisoners during the voyage. On the contrary they both speak to their advantage.'[11]

When she adjusted her vision to the glare of the southern sun and planted her shaky feet on the new continent, Charlotte Badger found a settlement in the process of formation. Scott told his mother, 'This is one of the wildest looking places ever was seen . . . the town is pretty large, at first sight you would take it for a camp the houses all straggling, all one storey and white.'[12] Another visitor, the naturalist François Péron, who arrived a year after the *Earl Cornwallis*, was more taken with the town than Scott, writing that '[w]e were completely astonished at the flourishing state in which we found this singular and distant establishment'.[13]

We cannot know Badger's reaction to her new surroundings, but she must have been struck by the differences between her new home and the one she had left behind. Like other new arrivals she would have had to cope with the strangeness of a land where Christmas came at the wrong time of the year and where even the stars in the sky were differently arranged. And in contrast to her former inland home, she was now a resident of a coastal town that stretched around the shore and up the surrounding hills, with the sea that she had spent months crossing acting as a permanent backdrop. But there must have been some similarities, too, particularly the close-quartered jumble of buildings that made up the majority of Sydney. The newness of Sydney obviously set it apart from Bromsgrove, but both places featured wooden buildings sitting cheek by jowl. On the eastern side of Tank Stream were the buildings that contained the halls of civil colonial power, including the governor's residence. The western side was altogether more unruly and included the area known as the Rocks, where the houses of the convicts sat together, sometimes clinging to the outcrops that gave the location its name. Around the wharf at the foot of the Rocks were warehouses belonging to traders who had done their time as convicts and worked to amass wealth of their own, while the slopes of Tank Stream became home to houses built by other prosperous former convicts such as Simeon Lord.[14] Meanwhile, because the new settlement proved a disappointing place for agriculture, ex-convicts and soldiers had taken up land out at Parramatta and on the Cumberland Plain, especially up the Hawkesbury River. They were joined by a government farm at Green Hills, now known as Windsor. All told around 6000 Europeans occupied these places by the beginning of the nineteenth century, a number that closely resembled the population of Bromsgrove and its surrounding parish.

On the other hand, the harshness of the physical environment was something entirely new. While the snow and ice of winter in the English Midlands had a brutality of their own, nothing could have prepared Badger for the southern summer that awaited her just a few months after arrival. It wasn't just the heat that would have floored her, dressed as she was for a northern climate; there were also the sudden, violent rainstorms that had the ability to stamp out the tender shoots that sprang from the foreign soil. Badger and her fellow convicts must have been disheartened to find that the food shortages and poor harvests they had suffered at home could blight their new lives, too. In the months leading up to her arrival, the settlers at the Hawkesbury had suffered what King called 'one of those calamities with which it pleases God sometimes to afflict mankind and which no human foresight can avoid' when no less than three floods inundated the area. Half the wheat crop and nearly all the corn had been destroyed, along with almost the entire pig population. The colony was able to call on the stores being sent from England, including salt meat brought by the *Earl Cornwallis*, but King still had to reduce colonists' rations by one-third before the next harvest or until more provisions arrived. By the end of the following year, the wheat crop had recovered, but drought had affected maize production during what King described as 'the most oppressive sultry weather ever felt here'.[15]

Adding to the anxiety around food supply was another aspect of life in the new settlement that Badger and her fellow Europeans had simply never encountered before: namely, the country's existing residents. From Sydney Cove's earliest days, tensions between the new arrivals and Aboriginal people flared into violence as convicts and soldiers encroached on land and resources. A series of raids and skirmishes in the first year of the colony had resulted in the deaths of an estimated four male convicts and led one nervous European inhabitant to write that 'the savages still continue to do us all the injury they can, which makes the soldiers['] duty very hard. . . . I know not how many of our people have been killed'.[16] As the settlement spread out over the Cumberland Plain in order to plant the crops it so desperately needed, episodes of direct conflict escalated, with Aboriginal warriors targeting maize for both removal and destruction by fire. This state of affairs had led to the almost-immediate founding of Parramatta as a garrison town, but the conflict kept coming. By 1801, when Badger arrived, a years-long campaign waged by Aboriginal leader Pemulwuy had unnerved and terrorised European settlers across the plain, leading them to fear not only for their crops but also for their lives. One estimate put the number of colonists killed during this period at twenty-six, with another thirteen wounded.[17] A lull in this guerrilla war followed Pemulwuy's death, but violence broke out again in 1805, putting the whole colony on edge.

But Aboriginal people were not just a threat lurking at the back of settlers' and convicts' minds; they were also neighbours. As Paul Irish put it, by the 1810s Aboriginal people from coastal areas 'had been frequent visitors to Sydney for two decades, calling on the governor, sleeping in dwellings with convicts, and doing odd jobs around town, and many European residents knew them by name. Aboriginal people also laid claim to spaces in the town such as Hyde Park to hold ritual combats.'[18] Of all the reminders of the distance Badger had travelled and the new land she now inhabited, perhaps the presence of these indigenous people, so different in appearance from anyone she had encountered before, was the most striking. She now stood on land, known by its original owners as Warrane, which would become the focus of negotiation, debate and outright conflict. And like other colonists, she would live with the consequences of that conflict for years to come.

But, for now, Badger's daily life was most immediately shaped by Sydney's role as a convict colony, the reason she was there in the first place. The idea of such a colony had been born in Whitehall and in the wake of revolution. Banishment of the troublesome, the dissolute and the incorrigible was not a new thing; Britain had used transportation of criminals as a way of supplying its colonies in North America with cheap labour throughout the eighteenth century, thereby also reducing the burden on the public purse that accommodating those people in the country's gaols would cause. But the war with colonists in America that had ended transportation there and made the stowing of prisoners in the hulks necessary also landed government officials with the task of deciding on a long-term alternative. The devastating loss of the colonies coincided with John Howard's exposé of the state of England's prisons and the proposal for penitentiaries where prisoners would be improved and reformed rather than strictly punished. This was an idea whose time was yet to come, though, as those in power continued to see the nation's criminals as largely beyond the reach of rehabilitation and in need of punishment rather than remedy. Criminality was a kind of moral failure that must be dealt with through harsh measures, including hard labour, which might deter the individual from further offending. In this view of the nation's offenders, there was little room for the occasional acts of clemency and humane practicality that had characterised the magistrates charged with overseeing Worcester County Gaol. Instead, the decision was made to find another destination to which to send the convicted where they could stave off the indolence that was seen as the root cause of their criminality. Consideration was given to establishing a convict colony on the south-west coast of Africa, but the idea was abandoned when scouting parties found no suitable, hospitable site. Thoughts then turned to a recommendation made by Joseph Banks, who had accompanied James Cook on his first voyage to the Pacific. Banks put forward Botany Bay as the ideal site for a convict colony, and once other options had been exhausted the decision was made. When Arthur Phillip arrived with the First Fleet in 1788, he found Banks's assessment to be overly optimistic and the site lacking in the promised arable pastures. Phillip and the convicts and marines in his charge relocated their settlement a few miles away through the headland of what became known as Port Jackson, and the future was set.

Whether through design or opportunity, Sydney quickly became more than just a dumping ground for Britain's human refuse. By the time of Badger's arrival it was also the administrative hub for satellite settlements at Norfolk Island and the soon-to-be-established Hobart Town, as well as a thriving port, sending and receiving vessels from across the world. The discovery of fur seal colonies off the southern coast of New Zealand and in what became known as Bass Strait gave rise to local merchants eager to dispatch shiploads of hunters to those windswept places and send the harvested furs to the Chinese or London markets. By 1810, eleven Sydney-based merchants had shipped cargoes mostly consisting of seal skins from New Zealand to Port Jackson.[19] Among them was Simeon Lord, who had built up a mercantile business selling goods brought in by visiting captains before buying vessels of his own and then going into partnership with others involved in the sealing trade.[20] Sealers were joined by the men of the 'world-wandering whaleships' sent mostly from London in search of the sperm whales off the Australian and New Zealand coasts.[21] Some of those whale ships had been used to bring convicts to New South Wales, including the *William and Ann*. This vessel, owned by Enderby and Sons of London, arrived in 1791 as part of the Third Fleet and was captained by Eber Bunker, who went on to become one of the first whalemen to hunt in New Zealand waters. While sealing voyages focused on New Zealand's southern seas, the hunt for whales took in the northern waters as well, with ships stopping at the Bay of Islands for refreshment before heading across the Pacific. By the first decade of the nineteenth century other goods were attracting the attention of these roaming vessels, including pork from Tahiti and sandalwood from Fiji.[22]

Péron gave a vivid account of the scene as all these vessels gathered at Sydney's waterfront:

> In the port we saw, drawn up together, a number of vessels that had arrived from different parts of the world, and most of which were destined to perform new and difficult voyages. Some of them had come from the banks of the Thames or the Shannon to pursue whale-fishing on the frigid shores of New Zealand. Others, bound to China after depositing the freight which they had received from the English government for this colony, were preparing to sail for the mouth of the Yellow River; while some laden with pit-coal, were about to convey that precious combustible to India and the Cape of Good Hope. Several smaller vessels were on their way to Bass's Straits to receive skins, collected by a few individuals who had established themselves on the isles of those straits to catch the marine animals that resort to them.[23]

Despite its status as a prison colony, Sydney was an outward-looking town, and the continual coming and going of ships must have reminded some of its inhabitants of their lack of freedom, as well as offering hope of eventual return home. Escape attempts were relatively common in Sydney's early years and could take a variety of forms, including absconding to the bush. Most escapees who wanted a permanent exit, though, saw the ocean as their best way of getting out, often stowing away on ships that called in on their voyages across the globe.[24] One such convict was Badger's former shipmate Frances Pounds, who was charged with attempting to flee the colony.

But those convicts who looked out to sea in hope did not do so from the confines of a gaol cell. In fact, the ability to attempt an escape was the result of the lack of restrictions placed on them and the relative freedom of movement they enjoyed. For all their legal servitude and status as captives, convicts in the first decades of settlement had an element of control over their lives, in respect of where they lived and the work they were expected to perform. The ceaseless toil that was supposed to fully occupy and punish the indolent simply did not exist. In contrast to the image of uniformed male prisoners from Hyde Park Barracks chained together clanking their way along George Street that presented itself to a Scottish visitor named John Webster in 1838, early convicts lived in their own or someone else's homes and created their own social spaces.[25] The military men who had been sent out to guard the colony in those early years did not see it as their job to oversee convict workers, so instead work was organised so that the settlement could be built and food could be grown without the punitive regulation of a prison. The men who inhabited the unruly houses in the Rocks spent their days working on building sites, at the brickworks, or at the lumberyard, laying down their tools in the mid-afternoon when the day's assigned tasks were done; their time was then their own to do with as they pleased. Even those who had been assigned to work for private masters or on the government farms at Parramatta and Castle Hill enjoyed leisure time. In 1804 Governor King published the list of tasks that convicts could be required to perform and the monetary value attached to them. A convict planting corn, for example, had to plant one and a half acres a week; the payment for each acre was 6s 8d.[26] If convicts worked overtime, they were entitled to be paid out in goods, and if a neighbouring farmer offered the convict extra work and a better pay rate he could choose to take it up. On the other hand, a convict who regularly failed to meet the minimum task requirements might face punishment.[27]

The leisure time afforded to convicts gave them the temporal space in which to build a new and sometimes riotous community, while the physical space was provided by the town's marketplaces and squares. Here, convicts could indulge in drinking, gambling and bare-knuckle fighting. Meanwhile, the more skilled and industrious were using their time to build small enterprises as blacksmiths, masons, painters and the like.

François Péron, who had been impressed by Sydney town, was also taken with the improving effect that life in the colony and the possibility of freedom and the acquisition of property had had on some of its inhabitants:

> The population of the colony was to us a new subject of
> astonishment and contemplation. Perhaps there never was
> a more worthy object of study presented to the philosopher
> – never was the influence of social institutions proved in a
> manner more striking and honourable to the distant country
> in question. Here we found united, like a family, those banditti
> who had so long been the terror of their mother country.
> Repelled from European society, and sent off to the extremity
> of the globe, placed from the very hour of their exile in a state
> between the certainty of chastisement and the hope of a better
> fate, incessantly subjected to the inspection as inflexible as it is
> active, they have been compelled to abandon their anti-social
> manners; and the majority of them, having expiated their

crimes by a hard period of slavery, have been restored to the
rank which they held amongst their fellow men.[28]

Not everyone's view was so optimistic. Ten years after the colony's
founding, David Collins, Sydney's unofficial historian, was lamenting
the crimes that continued to be committed by those already under
sentence, the escapes that were still being attempted and the
'turbulent and refractory' nature of recently arrived Irish prisoners
who were 'so dissatisfied with their situation that, without the most
rigid and severe treatment, it was impossible to derive from them
any labour whatsoever'.[29] In 1804 Collins's concerns about the
recalcitrant Irish erupted into life on the government farm beyond
Parramatta, at Castle Hill. In March that year convicts who had been
assigned to work there overpowered constables and other convicts
working as overseers and set about implementing a plan to take over
the colony. Their first taste of rebellion was successful, as they seized
arms from the farms at nearby settlements. By the time they got to
Parramatta they were about three hundred in number. From there
on, there was nothing but defeat. The expected uprising of convicts
at Parramatta did not eventuate, and following their retreat to the
Hawkesbury they were overwhelmed by a small party of soldiers.
The leader was summarily hanged and ten others were subsequently
sentenced to death, while another nine were flogged and thirty more
were dispatched to the penal settlement at Newcastle. Most of the
instigators of this failed revolt were Irish and had acted in the wake of
the Vinegar Hill uprising against English military presence in Ireland
in 1798.

This dichotomy between the improving possibilities of the new
land and the fear of entrenched criminality and potential violence
of the male convicts who made up the majority of those transported
to New South Wales was replicated when it came to the female
prisoners, but in a different way. By 1801 when Charlotte Badger
arrived, there were around 1500 women in Sydney, compared to

roughly 4300 men.[30] This was not the first time she had lived in an environment where she and her sisters were outnumbered; that had been a fact of life since the time she had been arrested and put in Worcester County Gaol. But living as a minority did nothing to diminish the alarm with which Badger and women like her were viewed by those charged with running the colony. As Portia Robinson has pointed out, men in authority always seemed more concerned with women's immorality than their criminality, and their judgment on this count was severe. Female convicts were 'women without shame or decency, women who would sell their bodies for a tot of spirits or a bottle of grog, who would lie and cheat, entice men to rob and thieve to satisfy their lust, women who plagued every governor, thwarted all attempts by colonial officials to promote marriage and to encourage morality among the inhabitants'. [31] Yet they were also expected from the very beginning to provide the homemaking services and childbearing that would give the settlement a semblance of stability and sustainability. The skills they brought with them, whether needlework, dressmaking, lacemaking, or the more mundane knowledge of how to cook and clean, would be vital in establishing the basis of colonial society.[32] Badger possibly brought these kinds of skills with her from her time working for Benjamin Wright, just as she brought the judgment that came from having broken into his house and stolen from him. Like other women, she was seen by those in authority as both a moral hazard and a necessary pillar of the new society.

This expectation of domesticity played out from the very moment she arrived in the colony. Even before she first stepped ashore she would have been sized up and assessed as a human chattel in short supply, as captured in this description from 1798:

> As soon as we came to an anchor the decks were crowded
> with gentlemen settlers and men convicts, who came, some to
> choose servants and some to choose wives, as they please to call

them. When those who were pitched upon were landed the others were taken in open boats up the river to a settlement called Parramatta. When they arrived there the gentlemen, after picking out those they wanted for different uses, gave the others their free will, to go with any man they chose.[33]

We do not know what happened to her when the men came on board the *Earl Cornwallis* to make their selections. In fact, we know next to nothing about what happened to Badger in the five years after she arrived in Sydney. We do not know if she found herself in the house of a marine officer or some other colonial official, making his meals and warming his bed. We do not know if she struggled by on government stores hoping for a more stable life. But we do know that on the day she arrived she met the criteria of being a typical female convict. Like most of the women transported to New South Wales, she was young and unmarried. She was also a first offender rather than a career felon, whose crime had involved stealing goods from someone she knew and who had been sentenced to a seven-year term as a result. As Deborah Oxley put it, 'These were casual criminals, many of whom committed their offences in familiar surrounds – at the shops, in lodgings, at work – and against familiar people. They stole from their masters and mistresses, other types of employers, and clients paying for laundry to be done or sexual services to be granted. Most appear to have acted alone.'[34] And, like most women, Badger did not appear before a New South Wales magistrate for committing a subsequent crime.

We also know which course Badger's early life in the colony was most likely to take. While some women were fortunate enough to live with respectable free families, acting as housekeepers and childminders, a larger number found themselves assigned to single men of low status. All up, by 1804 two-thirds of women still serving their sentences were living as wives in private houses.[35] As Kay Daniels has said, 'in the first two decades of the settlement in New

South Wales the majority of convict and ex-convict women lived in legal or de facto marriage relationships, and their work as servants was indistinguishable from their responsibilities as wives'.[36]

For unfortunate women, these relationships could become the road to penury if they broke down, especially if they produced children. As Daniels has put it, 'what we observe in this period is the beginning of the great Australian male habit of wife desertion. It was the women and children who were left in need of support.' The difficulty of the women's situation was compounded by the fact that their family support had been left behind in Britain: 'For many women the absence of kin meant a lack of protection afforded by fathers and brothers, an absence of the support offered by female relatives, and the assistance which came from wider kinship networks. It might also have meant severance from an economic unit as well as a social one.'[37]

However, these relationships were not necessarily oppressive or temporary. Some de facto couples could stay together for long periods: Sarah Bellamy, who arrived on the *Lady Penrhyn*, lived with James Bloodsworth until his death, while Elinor McDonald remained in a de facto relationship with Jonathan Griffiths until she died. While in some cases the decision to remain unmarried may have been the result of one or both of the partners already having a spouse in Britain, other such relationships were made formal. Elizabeth Berry, also known as Jessie, was assigned as a servant to Sergeant Charles Whelan. She lived with him until the two married in 1810. Ann Bryne, an Irishwoman transported in 1803, met Owen McMahon on her convict ship the *Rolla*. They became a de facto couple and by 1809 they had three children together. The next year, Owen went sealing, never to return. Three years later Ann had another child, and in 1815 she married the father, Richard Gilbert.[38] These relationships show a longevity and commitment, but they could offer women a measure of freedom and control. As Grace Karskens has argued, '[c]ouples lived more as partners, albeit in different spheres. It was normal for both men and women to work, to keep "separate chests" and have different circles of friends.'[39] When husbands became violent or failed to support their children, wives could and frequently did take them to court, and won.

Despite this potential for domesticity, women living in these relationships were not spared the opprobrium of the men in charge of the colony. Governor King reserved his harshest comments for those women reliant on government work, whom he described as 'of the worst description, and totally irreclaimable, being generally the refuse of London, very few of them are useful, except those employed spinning, who are mostly from the country'.[40] Samuel Marsden, the Church of England chaplain stationed at Parramatta, took a broader view. Although he pitied women who arrived in Sydney with no understanding of their new home and the perils that confronted them as they were picked over by unworthy men, he nevertheless blamed them for compromising the morality of the settlement:

> These unhappy exiles, by suffering every hardship that nature can bear and by living in habitual vice to procure a precarious subsistence lose every idea of propriety, morality and religion and exist merely to increase their own wretchedness and to corrupt society by their vicious examples. Being so unhappily situated and their past and present conduct being such, as not to bear a moment's reflection hence they banish from their minds all thoughts of a future state, neglect every moral, social and religious duty and live and die the most miserable of the human race.[41]

For Marsden, the ruination these women embodied was made worse by the fact that so many of them were already living in a state of what he considered prostitution. He claimed that there were around 1430 white women in New South Wales, of whom

1035 were unmarried, and he drew no line between those women who were in ongoing de facto relationships and those who had been abandoned. Instead, all of these women were counted as 'concubines' in the census of women that he conducted in 1806. No good could come from such unions, least of all their illegitimate progeny: 'These children, the offspring of unlawful connections and in general from the most vicious parents will unavoidably become a constant source of trouble, vexation and expense to the state.' Nothing less than the future of the colony was at stake if this situation continued: 'If the same immoral custom continues, public crimes and public calamities will increase in proportion to the number of inhabitants and also the public expense. One prodigal sometimes brings ruin upon a family and many prodigals will bring ruin upon a state.'[42]

In Marsden's mind the only possible remedy was marriage. This change in condition would prevent feckless men from having the option of abandoning one woman for another and would give women the stable base on which a life of moral rectitude might be built. As he explained, 'A woman who lives with a man as his mistress is aware that all she receives from him depends upon his whim and caprice and that he can dismiss her from his service at pleasure. Hence, she has no motive to industry and frugality because she has no permanent interest in the property which their joint exertions might acquire but on the contrary is under the strongest temptations to extravagance, and unfaithfulness.'[43]

As Portia Robinson argued, Marsden's complaints displayed a limited understanding of the social realities of the colony, pointing to the words of Governor King as evidence of a competing, more pragmatic view. The same year that Marsden composed his treatise on women convicts and conducted his census, King wrote to Lord Castlereagh informing him that of the 1413 white women in New South Wales, 1216 were living at no public expense and were either married or living with 'free people of all description'.

He also pointed out that 'their domestic concerns and providing for their families is an advantage to the society they are placed in' and that forcing men and women into marriage not only went against the idea of individual will but also threatened to debase the concept of marriage itself.[44] But Marsden's view of these women had a lasting impact. Not only did subsequent governors continue to see marriage as an answer to social ills, but the view of the women as 'damned whores' rather than contributors to the emerging colonial economy dominated the views of officials and contemporary commentators. The view became so engrained that even in 1837 it was asserted that '[t]he evil consequences arising to the colony from the indiscriminate association and the unrestrained prostitution of so many licentious women, have been seriously felt by the inhabitants at large'.[45]

Whether she ended up living with a man of high or low status, Charlotte Badger would have been branded as one of Marsden's vicious fallen women for the simple fact that at some point in the years immediately after arriving in New South Wales she had given birth to a child without marrying. In 1806 Badger was described in a public notice as being the mother to a young child. In what is the only known account of Charlotte Badger's appearance, she is described as follows: 'very corpulent, with full face, thick lips, and light hair, had an infant child'.[46] The reason for her appearance in that notice is the subject of the next chapter, but this shred of evidence is all we know for sure about her for five years, and it alone marked her as one of Marsden's 'concubines'.

But while being an unmarried mother was the clearest sign of her descent into what the colonial elite viewed as a life of vice, it is unlikely that that was the only aspect of Badger's behaviour that caused them concern. Like other working-class women, she probably exhibited the type of rough habits that offended their sensibilities. Many of Sydney's middle-class residents were unfamiliar with the manners of the working class and were shocked by the women's language and drinking habits and by the culture they embodied. The most audacious of the female convicts were 'possessed of short tempers and big mouths' and 'effectively used language to retaliate against and humiliate men'.[47] They inhabited public spaces and indulged in singing, dancing and fighting in the streets, abandoning what was seen as feminine respectability and embodying disorder.[48] These women tended not to be chosen to serve in the houses of the elite but ended up as the irredeemable participants in King's public work schemes. They were described as 'the disgrace of their sex', 'far worse than the men and . . . generally found at the bottom of every infamous transaction that is committed in the colony'.[49] They had violated the basic tenets of respectable womanhood at a time when the idea of respectability as a social marker was taking hold. That idea gripped Britain following the evangelical revival of the opening decades of the nineteenth century as Methodists and their evangelical Anglican counterparts stressed industry and sobriety as the central tenets of a Christian life. Respectable outward behaviour and self-control became part of the 'grammar of difference' that would separate middle-class and 'decent' members of the working class from the degenerate working class.[50] For women, the expectation of industry, particularly when it came to keeping a clean and orderly home and maintaining the domestic sphere, was coupled with the gendered expectations of docility, subservience and sexual virtue, so that they were doubly damned when they went astray.[51] In Sydney, extra measures would be needed to correct their particular vices.

In his treatise, Marsden had argued for a place where women might be taken and accommodated upon arrival while their 'respective characters and qualifications were ascertained and suitable situations and employments found for them'. Such a place opened around 1802 on the top floor of the new gaol at Parramatta. What King referred to as the 'manufactory' and what elsewhere was known as 'the factory above the gaol' acted as a clearing house for newly arrived women where the suitable could be assigned to work for settlers or as housekeepers, and where the unemployed and the 'incorrigible' could be put to work weaving cloth.[52] In a report published in 1822 this institution was described as follows:

> The factory itself . . . consists of one long room that is
> immediately above the gaol, having two windows in front that
> look into the gaol yard, one in the end of the building, and
> two windows looking into a yard that is immediately behind.
> The dimensions of the room are 60 feet by 20; and at one end
> are store-rooms, where the wool, yarn and cloth are kept.
> There is one fire-place, at which all the provisions are cooked.
> The women have no other beds than those they can make from
> the wool in its dirty state; and they sleep upon it at night, and
> in the midst of their spinning wheels and work. No attempt has
> been made to preserve cleanliness in this room, as the boards
> had shrunk so much, that when they were washed, the water
> fell through them into the prison rooms below. The walls of
> the room and the roof bore equal marks of neglect; and the
> drains in the yard were in the highest degree offensive.[53]

Charlotte Badger's life story as described in the Dictionary of New Zealand Biography has her living in what later became known as the Female Factory, although the lack of surviving documentation makes it impossible to confirm whether this was the case. One of the sources on which the Dictionary entry is based asserted that she was in the factory prior to assignment to Hobart in 1806, and it is possible that this was accurate given that it had opened several years earlier. But another source has her living at the factory 'shortly after her arrival'.[54] The Dictionary entry also refers to her status as a mother and claims that while she was there, she gave birth to her child. In 1815 Marsden described the factory as accommodating 150 women and 70 children, so it is possible that, if she was confined to the factory, she had a child with her.[55] But there is another possibility too. In 1821 the original factory was replaced by a new, larger structure designed by Francis Greenway, the convict architect behind many of Sydney's finest colonial buildings. It 'served a variety of functions, as a house of industry, and place of secondary punishment, as a lying-in hospital, a marriage market and a labour bureau', and included a hospital for expectant mothers.[56] It is possible, therefore, that this element of the Badger story was based on an assumption that the treatment offered to women in the factory's heyday, when the numbers of women housed there was at its peak, was also offered to women of Badger's generation. Again, we cannot say for certain that Badger did not spend time in the factory, but the basis on which that assertion has been made is questionable.

Nevertheless, the claim that she was consigned to the factory, while unproven, associated Badger with women who knew how to get themselves into serious trouble. As the years went on, and as the new Female Factory expanded the range of services it provided, the inmates themselves were divided into three classes, with the first-class women usually being new arrivals for whom the factory was a refuge while they awaited assignment to a master. They were given superior food and clothing and the most amenable work, and were available for selection as settler wives. Second-class women were undergoing some sort of probation, either because they had committed a minor crime while on assignment, because they had proven unsatisfactory servants or because they had become pregnant. They were not eligible for assignment until the blight on their character had been washed away. The women in the third class were, in effect, prisoners. These inmates were supposed to have committed serious secondary offences, but shouting abuse at an employer could be enough to sentence a woman to six weeks.[57] They were put to hard labour as punishment, and from 1826 suffered the stigma of having their heads shaved. The following year a group of them organised a mass breakout in protest at food shortages and only returned when they were rounded up by soldiers from the 57th Regiment.[58] They were, in short, such stuff as colonial administrators' nightmares were made on. Theirs was not the building that Badger would have lived in had she been confined to the factory, but the third-class incorrigibles damned the institution's reputation in perpetuity.

The troublesome women of the Female Factory's third class were not the majority of the colony's female convicts, even if they cast a long shadow over their sisters' moral standing. And while for the hardened third-class women life in the colony became a road to perdition, or at least short-term tribulation, for most women, day-to-day existence was more mundane, and somewhat more agreeable. Even so, better-behaved women or those better suited to the domestic life to which they had been allocated might still find themselves in trouble if the man with whom they were living died or deserted them, or if they were forced to leave an abuser. Their precarious situation would be compounded if they had children. Those without other work outside their former home might find themselves on government stores until something better came along.

This latter reality is the one that probably befell Charlotte Badger. We can be confident that Badger entered some sort of relationship, despite there being no evidence of her marrying, not only because this was the most common fate for female convicts, but because of her status as a mother. When speaking about the rest of Badger's life up to 1806, absence can perhaps be used as evidence, given that her non-appearance in any official record suggests that she at least evaded the attention of the authorities and conformed with Governor King's characterisation of most convict women as providing the foundation stones of the new community.

But by 1806, something had changed in Badger's life and the period of settled obscurity came to an end. Now alone, save only for her child, she set out on another perilous voyage to yet another unfamiliar destination. We do not know what happened to the relationship that had led to motherhood, but her status as a single woman put her on a path to a world of almost unimaginable strangeness.

The
Pirate

In January 1806 the colonial brig *Venus* entered Port Jackson at the end of a trip that saw it take its first significant place in history. The previous year it had left Sydney for Norfolk Island with a passenger on board: Matara, son of Te Pahi, a senior Hikutū chief who offered his home at Wairoa Bay in the northern Bay of Islands as a safe anchorage for visiting whalers. At Norfolk Island the *Venus* collected two nanny goats and two sows as presents for Te Pahi, and then carried on to the Bay to deliver both the son and the gifts. Te Pahi then asked that he and four of his sons be taken on board the *Venus* as it sailed back to Norfolk Island, so that he could go to Sydney and meet Governor Philip Gidley King, who had both shown hospitality towards Matara and arranged for the gifts to be sent home with him. But the voyage turned sour when the *Venus*'s captain, William Stewart, 'ill-treated his passengers and threatened to retain Te Pahi's eight-year-old son to pay for their passages'.[1] The Norfolk Island commandant 'rescued the boy and welcomed the visitors', before organising for them to sail to Sydney. As a result of this trip, King and Te Pahi went on to form 'the first reciprocal relationship ever established between New Zealand and the outside world'.[2]

Stewart, meanwhile, took his ship to the new sealing grounds at the 'Penantipodes', or the subantarctic islands south of New Zealand. According to one account, the *Venus* arrived to find three American crews already there, one of whom, working for Simeon Lord, was not about to share the bounty. Stewart responded by raising the British flag, which the Americans promptly tore down, and which in turn provoked a short but violent confrontation. Stewart and his men were forced to retreat, but their escape from danger was short-lived. When a sudden squall damaged the ship's rudder, it headed out to sea, leaving the hapless captain and his sealing gang behind.[3] On arriving back at Sydney, it was under the command of its first mate.

Later in 1806 the *Venus* again sailed into history, this time as a pirated ship on its final voyage. To begin with, the trip seemed straightforward. The vessel was commissioned by the colonial government to take supplies to the new and struggling settlements of Port Dalrymple and Hobart Town in Van Diemen's Land to relieve the distress of the small communities of soldiers, settlers and convicts caused by food shortages. When it set sail in April loaded with grain, flour and pork, along with other government stores, there was little to suggest that it was in jeopardy or that the voyage would end in disaster. By the end, members of its crew had taken the ship by force from Port Dalrymple and sailed it to the Bay of Islands, before it disappeared for good. Among the people caught up in this calamity was Charlotte Badger.

The roots of what became the *Venus*'s final, ruinous voyage lay in the personal conflicts that arose over the weeks it was at sea. The group of people who caused arguably the most dramatic event in Badger's life was led by a man not cut out for the job: Samuel Rodman Chace. An American who had been heavily involved in the sealing trade, particularly in Bass Strait, Chace was second-in-command on the *Venus* during its ill-fated trip to the subantarctic, and it had been his decision to leave Stewart and the other men behind. The new first mate was another American, Benjamin Burnet Kelly, who had first come to New South Wales on board the whaler *Albion* alongside Captain Eber Bunker, who had captained the first whaling expedition in New Zealand waters, in 1792. Other crew included Richard Edwards, the second mate; Joseph Redmonds, a seaman; an anonymous Malay cook; two cabin boys named Thomas Ford and William Evans; and five other unnamed crewmen. Also on board was a soldier named Richard Thompson, and four individuals identified as convicts: Badger, Catherine Hagerty, John William Lancashire and Richard Evans.

We know who was on board the *Venus* thanks to a public notice published soon after the ship was taken, requiring governors and officers in command of any British-controlled ports that the vessel might arrive at to take the offending parties into custody so that 'they may be brought to condign punishment'.[4] This notice offered one of the earliest descriptions of what happened to the *Venus* and who was responsible, but it was soon added to by other accounts and sightings. But although the fate of the *Venus* was the subject of early reports, the stories of what happened to the ship, to Badger and to her cohorts evolved dramatically as they were told and retold over the next two hundred years. What we have been left with is an accumulation of first- and second-hand accounts as well as fictionalised retellings. Stripping away the layers of these stories, both in terms of what took place on board the ship and what became of the protagonists, is not easy, and even then we are left with some enduring mysteries. Trying where possible to unravel those mysteries starts with examining the central players and asking what caused them to be on the ship for its final journey, before moving on to deconstructing the stories of the piracy itself, and its aftermath.

Answering these questions starts with trying to understand why Charlotte Badger was on her way to Van Diemen's Land in the first place. The Dictionary of New Zealand Biography claims she had been assigned as a servant to a settler in Hobart, but evidence of this is hard to find. The assertion itself can be traced back to *The Brown Frontier*, published in 1967. But the book's author, C. W. Vennell, offers no corroborating evidence, and he describes Badger as having been 'born in the slums of London' and beginning her 'career of crime as an adolescent pick-pocket', which casts doubt on his reliability.[5] These claims of Badger's origins and assignment also appear in an earlier, highly fantastical article published in the *Sydney Morning Herald* in 1937, described further below, and it is probable that this was the source of Vennell's assertion.[6]

Despite these problems, there are good reasons for thinking that the story about her being sent to Hobart to work is plausible. Firstly, women were indeed being assigned to Van Diemen's Land. Both the first and second parties to establish European settlements in Van Diemen's Land, in 1803 and 1804, had included convict women. They were followed in 1805 by a group of women who had been transported on the *Experiment*. Also in 1805, Maria Risley, who had been convicted of theft and transported to Sydney the previous year, was selected by marine officer Edward Lord to accompany him to Hobart as his domestic servant.[7]

Secondly, despite the fact that Badger should have completed her sentence in 1803 and therefore no longer been subject to assignment three years later, there was often a delay in the expiration of a convict's sentence and the point at which they received their certificate of freedom. The certificate proclaimed that the recipient was 'restored to all the rights and privileges of free subjects', and as John Hirst has said, it was 'made necessary because in a society of convicts an ex-convict needed a ready means of indicating that he was a free man [*sic*]'.[8] They were not automatically issued once a sentence had expired, though, and convicts often had to take it upon themselves to apply. As a result, there could be significant delays in certificates being issued. Charles Wood, who was convicted at the same Worcester Assizes session as Badger in 1796 and then transported on the *Barwell*, was not given his official freedom until 1811, eight years after his sentence ended. The same was true for women who sailed on board the *Earl Cornwallis* with Badger. Frances Hoggard, Dinah Craddock, Sarah Mugford, Sarah Trapnell, Elizabeth Hicks, Sarah Robinson and Mary Franklin were also given their certificates of freedom in 1811, ten years after arriving in New South Wales, while Elizabeth Howe and Lydia Parker received theirs in 1810. Charlotte Jennings had to wait until 1826. In reality, receiving a certificate of freedom might not have made a lot of difference to a convict's daily life, especially if they were a female domestic servant or a wife serving out her sentence in her own home. This would help explain why these women were not motivated to apply for freedom at the time it became available. There is no record of when Badger officially received her freedom, but given the frequency with which other women waited years to receive theirs, it is possible that she was still officially classed as a convict in 1806 when the *Venus* sailed because, in the absence of action, she had not been reclassified otherwise.

There is, of course, the possibility that Badger had been freed from servitude and was going to Van Diemen's Land of her own free will, but this is undercut by the dangers that such a decision would bring. In 1810 out of a population of 1321 there were twenty-three female convicts; in the convict population men outnumbered women ten to one.[9] A few years later it was still a place where '[v]iolence and oppression were widespread' and 'the few adult females were extremely vulnerable' and dependent on the protection of men, even if their small numbers gave them some leverage in selecting the men from whom they received that protection.[10] Given these risks, leaving the now-familiar surroundings of Sydney and going to the unknowns of Van Diemen's Land seems to defy explanation, especially when we remember that she was the mother of a young child.

A final possible explanation is that Badger was being sent to Van Diemen's Land because she had committed subsequent offences, and was being removed from Sydney as punishment. Van Diemen's Land was used as a place of secondary punishment, even for women,[11] but as stated in the previous chapter, there is no evidence that she came before a magistrate in the years following her arrival in New South Wales.

When all of this is considered, the most likely reason Badger was on her way to Van Diemen's Land is that she was going to be someone's servant. Perhaps, like Maria Risley, she was going to work for a military officer, or perhaps she had found herself on government stores after the relationship with her child's father had ended, and assignment to Hobart Town was one of the few options available that gave her a way out of that situation. Joining her on that journey were two other convicts who would play central roles in her life over the coming months, John William Lancashire and Catherine Hagerty, both of whom had their own, curious reasons for being on board.

Of all the people Badger sailed with, Lancashire is perhaps the easiest to get a handle on, thanks to his regular appearances in the courts. Described as being 'about 5 feet 4 inches high, sallow complexion, brown hair, a little marked with the small pox, of an emaciated appearance', by his own account he had started life as 'a youth of honest, respectable, and worthy parents who ever lived in affluence'. His life story suggested he did not follow their example. He claimed that, as a boy, he had served as a captain's clerk in the Royal Navy, before ill health forced him to leave. Given the Royal Navy's role as 'a familiar reform school of the era for errant sons and nephews', this might have been the first sign of the life that lay ahead.[12] After being discharged, he worked for his uncle, a banker, in London 'for some considerable time'. At this point, it seems, whatever grip on respectability he might have had gave way, and in 1796 he was convicted in the Old Bailey on charges of feloniously stealing four pieces of linen from a shop in Fleet Street and was sentenced to seven years' transportation. He was twenty-two years old at the time of his crime, making him four years older than Badger when she was convicted the same year.[13] He then spent time in Newgate Prison, before being sent to Woolwich and held on board the *Stanislaus*, one of the hulks, or decommissioned warships, that served as temporary holding pens for convicts awaiting their journey to the Australian colonies. These floating gaols had first been used to relieve the strain on overcrowded prisons that resulted from the ending of transportation to North America with the War of Independence, but they continued to provide a cost-effective option even after New South Wales was pressed into service as the new penal colony.

After a year on the hulk, Lancashire was sent to New South Wales on board the *Barwell*, arriving at Port Jackson in May 1798. Once freed from the stifling, close-quartered captivity of the previous two years, he almost immediately set out on the dedicated crime spree that characterised much of his time in Sydney. By October he was arrested on suspicion of stealing, and by April of the following year he was in prison on charges of uttering a forged note. He was found guilty and sentenced to death, but pleaded his case to Governor Hunter, claiming he was innocent of the crime and hoping that 'your Excellency (I trust to the Almighty) will find something favourable in my behalf that my life might be spared and not cut off in the blooming flower of youth'.[14] It worked. Hunter granted a reprieve pending a decision from the king, but by the time Lancashire received a conditional pardon in June 1802, he was only weeks away from being arrested again, this time for theft. In one swift action he took pork from a Mrs Paton at the same time as offering her bottles that he had stolen from the hospital, and to which he was supposed to be affixing labels. He was sentenced to three months at Castle Hill farm and one hundred lashes. While there, he was further charged with illegally taking government stores, although he was acquitted for lack of evidence.

In between his repeated encounters with the law, Lancashire also set himself up as a draughtsman and a painter, of houses, ships and signs, as well as landscapes. His one surviving artwork is of a view of Sydney from the Rocks, completed in 1804 and now held by the State Library of New South Wales. A description of its qualities suggests that his real talent lay somewhere other than landscapes: 'Its rather static quality is highlighted by the artist's inability to convey any sense of depth, but the sharp focus and bright colours give it an almost hypnotic intensity.'[15] Although, perhaps not unsurprisingly, Lancashire did not make his fortune from his art, he did well enough for himself to become the owner of a house and adjoining property in Parramatta.

In the end it was Lancashire's repeated charges of forgery rather than his artistic skills that led to his name being written into history's pages. By the middle of 1803, he was back before the court under indictment for the same crime that had seen him facing a death sentence only four years earlier. This time he was found not guilty, but Elizabeth Fielder, with whom he was living, was convicted and gaoled. His luck held several years later when, in early 1806, he was again facing charges of forgery, this time relating to a promissory note, but was again acquitted. At this point he went too far by counter-charging his gaolers with cruelty. The bench was not convinced by his pleadings and found that 'from the prisoner's notoriously bad character, and having once broke out of gaol, he had not been treated with inhumanity'.[16] The court's judgment was echoed by Governor King himself, who described Lancashire as being 'possessed of every art of cunning that human nature could turn to the worst of purposes'.[17] The authorities' suspicions about Lancashire were confirmed when in April he tried to escape the colony on board the *Tellicherry*.[18] He was sentenced to work for the government for three years, and one hundred lashes. By June he was being removed from Sydney altogether and sent to Van Diemen's Land on board the *Venus* to join the small community of convicts and soldiers that had been founded on the Derwent River two years earlier.

Other than Lancashire, the person on board the *Venus* whose story intersected most closely with Badger's was Catherine Hagerty, perhaps the most enigmatic and unknowable character in Badger's life. Originally from Ireland, Hagerty was transported on board the coincidentally named *Kitty* in 1792 for an unknown crime. Once in Sydney she formed a relationship with a man named Richardson, with whom she had a son, Henry, born in November 1793. By the next year, though, Richardson was off the scene, and Catherine went to work as a domestic servant for Richard Atkins, one of the colony's best-known judges. (Atkins had heard the case against Lancashire when he was charged with taking government stores.) In 1795, Hagerty and Atkins had a daughter together, named Theresa.

Atkins kept a journal during his time in New South Wales and devoted almost interminable space to ruminations on the physical environment and moral philosophy but did not spare a line for his daughter and made only one brief mention of Catherine, or Kitty, during the six years she lived with him. Perhaps this is not surprising given the nature of their relationship and Theresa's status as a child born outside marriage to a supposedly respectable man of high standing. It took the end of the relationship for Atkins to acknowledge Catherine in writing, when she was granted a full pardon in 1800. She left the colony immediately afterwards, taking Henry with her but leaving Theresa behind with her father. On 26 February 1800 Atkins wrote, 'Kitty left me, went on board the Relliance with her son for England.'[19] The HMS *Reliance*, a government ship, was being sent home in a dilapidated state while it could still make the journey.

The obvious question is, if Hagerty left New South Wales in 1800, then how could she have been on the *Venus* six years later? This is a question without a straightforward answer. There is no record of Catherine Hagerty being sent back to New South Wales as a convict or of her being given permission to return there as a free settler. Several years later a young man named Henry Atkins appeared on a list of people who had been granted permission to travel as free settlers from England to New South Wales. In his case, the reason given for the request was so that he could 'Return to his Father'.[20] It is possible that this was Hagerty's son applying to return to his stepfather, perhaps because his mother had died or was unable to care for him because of illness. But the only clue suggesting that Henry went back to live with Richard Atkins in New South Wales is an 1806 census that lists Atkins's new wife as having charge of an illegitimate son, so even this cannot be taken as a clear sign of Hagerty's fate.[21]

In other words, there is no way, simple or otherwise, to explain why Catherine Hagerty was listed as being on board the *Venus*. Yet, in the absence of another explanation, we have to accept that she was the woman described in the public notice as 'middle-sized, light hair, fresh complexion, much inclined to smile, and hoarse voice'.

Another remaining mystery that surrounds Hagerty is the nature of her prior relationship with Badger. The Dictionary account of Badger's life has her meeting Hagerty in the Female Factory and being assigned to Hobart together. While this possibility cannot be entirely dismissed, as argued in the previous chapter there is no real evidence to suggest that Badger spent time in what would have been called the 'manufactory' before 1806, and therefore there is also no firm basis for thinking that she and Hagerty were anything other than strangers when they set foot on board the *Venus*.

Together, these three people, Badger, Lancashire and Hagerty, flung together by the trajectories of their separate lives, found themselves on a shared voyage towards an uncertain future. Along the way they became part of a group from all over the globe, a 'motley crew' of sailors and then mutineers. Like many ships from the mid-seventeenth century onwards, when the need for maritime labour to work the ships of Britain's nascent commercial and naval empire rapidly increased, the *Venus* was a world contained. Among its crew were the American Kelly, the unnamed Malay cook, the 'Mulatto' sailor Joseph Redmonds, described as having 'holes in his ears, being accustomed to wear large earrings', as well as English sailors and convicts, and a cabin boy who was 'a native of this Colony'.[22] Ships like these have been described as 'a meeting place where various traditions were jammed together in a forcing house of internationalism'. In the cramped, sweaty world below decks, men (and some women), Herman Melville's 'mongrel renegades', could develop a kind of situational solidarity born of shared experience and interests.[23] On the *Venus*, too, relationships formed and interests converged, with disastrous consequences for all involved, including the man at the centre of the debacle: the ship's master, Samuel Rodman Chace.

On 17 June, just after the ship disappeared, Chace gave a deposition at Yorkton, Van Diemen's Land, describing what had happened to his vessel.[24] According to his account, after leaving Sydney the *Venus* made for Twofold Bay, on the south coast of New South Wales, where it stayed for just under five weeks. The reason for this extended stay, particularly when the vessel had convicts and essential supplies on board, is unclear, but it is possible that Chace was interested in finishing the salvage of the ironwork from the wrecked schooner *George*, which he had started in March.[25] The layover at Twofold Bay, though, witnessed the beginnings of the trouble that dogged the *Venus* throughout its journey to Van Diemen's Land as tensions on board mounted. Goods began to go missing, which Chace blamed on the crew and 'other persons on board'. When he accused Kelly of taking a cask of liquor Kelly denied it, but the damage to the relationship was done. Things quickly deteriorated to the point where Chace believed 'the vessel was in danger of being run away with', and he asked the master of the *Marcia*, then also moored at the bay, upon his return to Sydney to inform the agent of the *Venus*'s owner that 'from the general behaviour of the people on board he [Chace] did not believe the vessel safe'. Chace also told the *Marcia*'s captain that 'in case a colonial vessel came into the Bay he would give up the brig to her, as the crew were robbing and plundering the vessel, and he did not think his life safe'. Nonetheless, instead of returning to Sydney, in early June the *Venus* continued on its voyage to Port Dalrymple. If Chace thought that putting to sea would calm the crew's recalcitrance then he was mistaken. At this point in the account, Catherine Hagerty, who was apparently cohabiting with Kelly, made her first querulous appearance when she threw a box of papers overboard. Chace turned the ship about, but it was too late to retrieve the box.

On 16 June the *Venus* anchored at the head of the Tamar River near Port Dalrymple, and Chace went on shore to deliver dispatches to the lieutenant-governor. He then went on board the schooner *Governor Hunter*, where he stayed overnight. Perhaps he needed respite from the conflict that had taken over his ship, but his decision to leave the crew to its own devices was rightly criticised by Governor King as 'most imprudent and unjustifiable', especially given what came next.[26] The following morning, Chace went downriver to rejoin the ship, but instead he saw that it was under way. Five members of the crew came and found Chace and told him that Kelly, Evans and Thompson had overwhelmed and confined the second mate, Edwards, before forcing them off the ship. Kelly was armed with a musket and Evans with a pistol. The ship had then headed out to sea with Thompson at the helm.

What is missing from Chace's account is any explanation for why the crew turned on him. His version of events includes the unstated but clearly implied reasoning that he was simply unfortunate enough to end up with a bunch of ruffians whose behaviour caused the voyage to degenerate into chaos. The reality was probably far more complicated. Studies of British and American sailors during the late eighteenth and early nineteenth centuries, including those men serving on convict transports, have noted their reluctance to submit to 'poor working conditions and the infringement of their perceived rights'. Influenced by contemporary ideas of liberty, sailors would revolt against floggings and food shortages, and against the perceived tyranny of the captain. And in a repetition of history that must have truly terrified authorities, similar ideas had also driven pirates and mutineers in the Atlantic and Caribbean slave trade during the so-called 'Golden Age of Piracy' in the early years of the eighteenth century.[27] By 1806, uprisings had taken place on a number of convict ships, including the *Prince of Wales* and the *Royal Admiral*, over unfair treatment. What happened on board the *Venus* is consistent with these episodes in that discontent about provisions, coupled with the captain's handling of complaints, led to disaster. According to Chace, tensions rose following the confrontation between himself and Kelly over the cask of liquor. Were the crew being denied what they saw as their rightful due and therefore helping themselves to the cargo meant for the officers of Van Diemen's Land?

The defiance of authority that underpins both the *Venus* mutiny and uprisings on board convict transports goes beyond theoretical similarities when it comes to one of the mutineers. Richard Evans, also known as Thomas Evans and David Evans, had come to New South Wales in 1804 as a sailor on HMS *Calcutta*, when it deposited 292 convicts at Sydney. He promptly deserted but 'was allowed to serve on board the [government ship] Lady Nelson with a promise that if his future Conduct merited it, application would be made in his favour'.[28] Any cursory effort Evans made to stick to the straight and narrow ended when he was found stealing from the *Investigator* and was sentenced to fourteen years. He now found himself heading to Van Diemen's Land as a convict, but he was also apparently acting as the *Venus*'s pilot.

Evans personified what authorities feared most: that sailors and convicts might unite. Given that most sailors and convicts were drawn from the same social class, and that a disproportionate number of convicts were former sailors, there was always a threat that they would see their interests as being more closely aligned with each other than with the men in charge of vessels.[29] What's more, both groups knew what it was like to live under the eye of a watchful ruler – either captain or governor. As David Haines and Jonathan West have put it, 'Lives inside colony and ship were each constrained by harsh, often brutal discipline and surveillance, provoking the same urge to resist, escape or otherwise seek freedom from authority.'[30] On board the convict transport *Hillsborough* this sense of shared interest had seen twelve seamen decide to desert even before the ship left port, and then inform the convicts of the plan so that they might 'seize such a favourable Opportunity' to escape. Two years earlier, both convicts and crew had plotted against the tyrannical captain of the *Britannia*.[31] On the *Venus*, Evans and Kelly, who was offside with his own captain, may have shared a sailors' sense of grievance that led them to joint action. Their willingness to act may have appealed to Thompson, who, as a soldier, belonged to a group that had shown a willingness to join with their sailor brothers to overthrow captains of convict ships on which they were acting as guards.[32] At the same time, Evans's experience as a runaway gave him something in common with Lancashire, who had tried to escape the colony on board the *Tellicherry*. And like Lancashire, he was being sent to Van Diemen's Land as a punishment for repeat offending. As the situation on board the *Venus* deteriorated, these two motivations, the overthrow of authority and escape, could have given each group, crew and convicts, reason to join forces.

For the other convicts on board, escape might not have been on their minds as they got on the ship, but they might have been willing to go along with the chance to leave servitude behind when the possibility presented itself. Although, as in the case of the *Venus*, soldiers and sailors sometimes made a run for it, a large majority of people who fled New South Wales were, unsurprisingly, convicts.[33] And although some of those convicts headed inland, most looked to the sea as their route to freedom. They must have known that the

odds of success were low and that most escape attempts ended in
failure. They also must have known that they could suffer flogging
and hard labour if they were caught, assuming the sea didn't claim
them first. But there were success stories, too. Runaways from
New South Wales made it to places across the globe, including
Calcutta, and some of them became famous. In 1791 Mary Bryant
had escaped the colony with her husband, William, her two
children and seven other convicts in the governor's small cutter.
They made it to Timor before being captured and taken in irons to
Batavia, where Mary's husband and son died. She and the remaining
escapees were then put on a ship for England. During the trip Mary
lost her daughter, too, but she and the four remaining convicts were
treated mercifully by the English authorities, and she ended her days
at home in Cornwall. As news of the story reached New South
Wales, that clemency was not appreciated by Governor Hunter,
who blamed it for a series of subsequent escape attempts.[34]

Like the Bryants' escape, most getaways were planned, collective
actions rather than individual rushes of blood to the head. When they
decided to go, runaways usually went together. As Marcus Rediker
has argued, 'escape was characterised by cooperation between people
of the same rank, by shared planning and decisions, and must have
involved a level of trust between escapees and those who helped
them, and within the groups themselves.'[35] Mutiny, in particular, was
a collective effort; no one individual could manage it alone. In the
case of the *Venus*, it is of course possible that Badger, Lancashire and
Hagerty were unwilling observers caught up in events beyond their
control and against their wishes. Badger and Hagerty, in particular,
might have been shut out of the decisions that led to the mutiny.
As a general rule, women who escaped with bands of men were
unlikely to have been included in the 'shared plans, codes and signals'
that preceded an escape attempt, so perhaps events moved quickly
without their knowledge and consent.[36] But Hagerty, at least, played
an active role in the unruly behaviour designed to undermine Chace's

authority, and her relationship with Kelly not only gave her a reason to go along with his actions, but might also have acted as a flashpoint for the uprising itself. On board the *Lady Shore* in 1797, 'attempts to prevent soldiers and crew from gaining access to the convict women' had soured relations with those in charge, and 'given the extent to which relationships had developed between the crew and their convict charges', it is likely that the women had been privy to the conspiracy that led to the only successful seizure of a convict transport.[37] If a similar dynamic had developed on the *Venus* and Kelly's cohabitation with Hagerty had become a point of conflict with Chace, then Hagerty would have had good reason to turn against the captain.

What we do know is that neither she nor Badger were put on the boat back to shore once the mutiny was under way. When presented with a chance to escape they were willing to take it, even if they might not have wielded the pistols. The extent to which this was an active rather than a passive decision is impossible to tell. Perhaps, already facing an unknown future in Van Diemen's Land, they saw this as a way of taking some measure of control over their destiny, even if the outcome was uncertain. Or perhaps the course of their lives had resigned them to fate's capricious hand. As Grace Karskens has said of New South Wales's early convicts, 'these were people whose worldview revolved about fate and opportunity: they were highly mobile, they took risks and they were resigned when disaster struck.'[38]

Nevertheless, Chace's account makes clear who was directly responsible for the overthrow of order on board and the eventual seizure of the vessel, and in this telling Badger is absent, at least as an active participant. But this first-hand description of events did not prevent her role from being bolstered in retellings in years to come. As the story developed, passivity gave way to instigation, so that by the twentieth century she was a central protagonist, and a pirate. The process of transforming Badger into a pirate that had begun with naming her as party to the 'piratical seizure' described in the public notice was carried forward by Louis Becke, an Australian whose life reads like an adventure story all of its own. After a career that took him across the Pacific as a 'blackbirder', beachcomber, trader, whaler, cattle drover and bank clerk, among other things, he turned to writing to make a living, mostly of the fictional kind but incorporating aspects of his own Pacific experiences. The story of the *Venus* appeared in *Rídan the Devil and Other Stories*,[39] an 1899 collection in which 'Becke started his custom of presenting volumes in which stories and non-fiction sketches and reminiscences were intermingled'.[40] At one point he describes Badger and Hagerty as 'entertaining Mr. Kelly . . . with a dancing exhibition' while the rest of the convicts and some of the crew lay around the deck in various states of drunkenness. When it came to the mutiny itself, Becke retained Kelly as the main instigator but promoted the women to co-conspirators who took part in overwhelming the helpless, loyal members of the crew armed with swords and pistols. Charlotte played a lesser role than Catherine, or Kitty, who was described as Kelly's partner. In a scene resplendent with imagined dialogue, Becke has Kelly take Kitty by the waist and say 'look at the pirate's bride', followed by much laughter from Kitty herself.[41]

Some forty years later an article entitled 'Australia's Only Woman Pirate' appeared in the Women's Supplement of the *Sydney Morning Herald*. This time, Charlotte was the star of the show, and her co-star, Catherine Hagerty, had not just been downgraded to a bit part, but had been written out altogether. In this telling, Charlotte took Kitty's part as Kelly's partner in crime, while the role of the quieter, less prominent female player was taken by a convict by the name of Sarah Barnes. The crew and passengers again descended into drunkenness, but this time the captain responded by putting all the participants, including the two women, in irons. This poor treatment instilled in Charlotte a desire for revenge, 'so she formed her plans for capturing the ship with the help of the mate as the Venus sailed down the coast'. After Kelly freed her and the other convicts, he handed out weapons. From this point on, the story leaves its readers with no doubt as to who was really in charge. 'Led by Charlotte Badger, the mutineers forced the crew and the remaining prisoners into the ship's boat, Charlotte herself thrashing the captain.' Her role as ringleader continued after the ship was taken out to sea: 'Kelly was navigator, but Charlotte Badger was in command, the two women taking their turn at watch on deck with the four men as the undermanned brig tossed across to New Zealand. Both women donned men's clothing and worked with the men, setting sail and steering the brig during this nightmare voyage across the Tasman Sea.'[42]

These retellings, as well as adding to the romanticism of Badger's life, have formed the basis of portrayals of her in everything from popular fiction to scholarly histories. The *Sydney Morning Herald* story has played an outsized role in this regard. It is the source of the idea, repeated in books such as *The Brown Frontier* and *Coasts of Treachery*, that she was a London pickpocket and career criminal, as well as the enduring myth that she was a pirate. Perhaps the most influential recent repetition of these ideas is the one that appears in the Dictionary of New Zealand Biography. Although Mary Louise Ormsby's entry on Badger in the Dictionary acknowledged that the stories about her role in the uprising on the *Venus* varied, it still recounted the version of her as a major protagonist without tracing its origins: 'According to one [account], she dressed in male clothing and, armed with a pistol, flogged the captain and conducted a raid on another vessel to obtain supplies and weapons. In another she and Catherine Hagerty are said to have incited the male convicts to rebel.' The Dictionary entry also claimed that Chace 'found the crew in a state of intoxication while the two women entertained them with a dance'.[43] Chace's testimony in the *Sydney Gazette* does not, in fact, claim this, but Becke's version and the popular history entitled *A Century of Our Sea Story*, which the Dictionary entry relied on as a source, did.[44]

Badger's inclusion in the Dictionary had two effects: it brought her to greater prominence, and it meant that the myths at the heart of that story spread further. But the same ideas that fuelled this imaginative rendition made their way into New Zealand's written histories too. A few years after the biography first appeared, James Belich retold her story in his general history of New Zealand, *Making Peoples*, using the Dictionary as a source and mixing it with other, earlier stories:

> One remarkable story among many was that of Charlotte Badger, a London pickpocket transported to Sydney in 1801. In 1806, she and her friend Kitty Hagerty were sent to Hobart in the brig *Venus*. The first mate Benjamin Kelly fell in love with Hagerty and fell under the strong-willed Badger's influence. Together they mounted a mutiny and seized the ship. Badger is said to have flogged the captain before forcing him ashore.[45]

More recently, Barbara Brookes was more circumspect in her *History of New Zealand Women*, noting that accounts of Badger's involvement in the *Venus* rebellion varied, but echoing the Dictionary's claim that Badger wore a man's clothing, flogged the captain and raided another vessel for supplies.[46]

The versions of her story found in places such as the *Sydney Morning Herald* have found their way into both works of fiction and non-fiction because each time that story is retold the layers have been built one on top of the other, and in the process the line between storytelling and history-writing has blurred. If those layers are stripped away, we are left with a story that is both less fantastical and less complete. We simply do not know the full extent of Badger's involvement in the rebellion on the *Venus* because the only contemporaneous report we have is from a man, Rodman Chace, who was not there at the time. We are left, instead, with doubt and questions and a type of historical lacuna. But what we can say is that the stories told and repeated about her being 'Australia's Only Woman Pirate' are built on shaky, porous ground that does not bear the weight of all that has been piled on top of it. This admission might be disappointing for storytellers and readers alike, but when we return to the bare bones of the reported account, we find a woman, and the mother of a young child, caught up in an act of violence, heading for a strange destination on the open ocean, and surely that is excitement enough.

After heading away from the safety of the coast the *Venus* soon entered the Tasman Sea, a mercurial body of water described as 'the best of seas and the worst of seas'.[47] Lucky sailors might strike it on a placid day; less fortunate ones might find themselves being carried on huge swells or battered by winds and assaulted by waves. In winter, when exposed to the full force of a prevailing sou'wester, it could more than earn its place in the Roaring Forties. The challenge of confronting the Tasman head-on and seeing the ship to safety in all likelihood fell to Benjamin Burnet Kelly, one of the lead mutineers and the highest-ranking member of the crew. The chaos of the mutiny could have seen the *Venus* head for immediate disaster if a disunited crew had fought amongst themselves over what to do and where to go. Fortunately, Kelly's travels on board the *Albion* had taken him to New Zealand, and there he would have experienced the hospitality, food and shelter to be gained at the Bay of Islands. Kelly might have seen the Bay as offering a bolt-hole with the necessities of life for himself and Hagerty away from the New South Wales authorities. And it was most likely his skill that saw the *Venus* navigate the three-to-four-week trip across the stretch of water that stood between them and their chosen destination.

But Kelly's success was temporary, as the mutiny began to splinter and crack. By the time they reached the Bay, fractures had opened up among the crew that had devastating consequences for all those on board, and for the boat itself.

The
Beach
Crosser

It is easy to understand Rangihoua pā's value as a citadel. From the top of the hill on which it was situated, the northern Bay of Islands, or Pēwhairangi, opened up so that the observer could see all approaching vessels. Any hopeful invaders would need to not only avoid the defender's eye but also overcome the ditches and palisades built to keep them out. It was a site worth defending. Looking east was the beach at Oihi, while to the west was the Te Puna valley, and beyond that Wairoa Bay, which provided safe harbours and landing places, as well as areas of flat land suitable for occupation and cultivation. The sea in front offered a wealth of kaimoana (seafood); the forest behind a bounty of birds and berries for eating and wood for building. So precious was the site in heavily populated Pēwhairangi that Rangihoua pā was only one of several defensive installations, with others on the nearby headland of Papuke and on the islands just offshore at Wairoa Bay.

For hundreds of years Māori grew crops and harvested both the land and sea here, sometimes trading with people from as far away as Te Wai Pounamu (the South Island). By the end of the eighteenth century the leading figure was Te Pahi of the Hikutū hapū, after whom one of the nearby islands was named, and who based himself at the village at Wairoa Bay and the adjacent islands. It was Te Pahi's fate to be the leader here when the outside world came calling. James Cook had visited Pēwhairangi on his first voyage to the Pacific on board the *Endeavour* in late 1769. In his journal Cook recorded that he had labelled the area the Bay of Islands, but the name meant nothing to the people who lived there and held no power over them, at least not to begin with. It wasn't until Cook's superiors in the Royal Navy and the British government established a permanent presence at Sydney Cove that the tentacles of European expansion began to curl themselves around the people of Wairoa Bay and the surrounding islands and settlements.[1]

That process began almost as soon as Sydney became a dot on an imperial map. Shortly after the First Fleet arrived in 1788, Philip Gidley King was dispatched to Norfolk Island to establish an outpost as commandant, partly to deter French interest in the Pacific. Once there he immediately began assessing the island's timber and set convicts to work on flax as a way of supplementing the navy's supplies of masts and rope. Norfolk flax proved an unyielding material, though, and the scheme foundered. But King was determined. On a trip home to England in 1791, and following consultation with Joseph Banks, he formed a scheme to bring flax dressers from New Zealand to Norfolk Island to unlock the secrets of how to produce straw from the native plant, which thrived in both locations. In 1793 the plan was put into action when the naval ship *Daedalus* seized two young men, Tuki Tahua and Huru Kokoti, offshore from Matauri Bay and took them to Norfolk Island via Port Jackson. Unfortunately, dressing flax was the province of women, meaning that Tuki and Huru were unhelpful teachers, and King eventually took them home, along with gifts of axes, spades, hoes, knives and scissors, bushels of maize and wheat, pigs and potatoes. Of all these gifts perhaps the last had the most important short-term effect as potatoes began to be grown in Te Tai Tokerau as a way of attracting and supplying the whaling ships that were beginning to visit New Zealand waters. These were, quite literally, the seeds from which ongoing Māori contact with Europe and the world beyond grew, and Te Pahi became an early and enthusiastic cultivator.

Around a year before the *Daedalus* had taken Tuki and Huru, another ship, the *William and Ann*, captained by Eber Bunker, had sailed to the north of New Zealand in search of whales. Bunker had been asked to collect flax dressers during his trip, but unlike the captain of the *Daedalus* he had demurred at the thought of taking Māori against their will. It is unclear whether he had any more luck finding whales.[2] It then took another decade before New Zealand waters became a regular hunting ground for whale ships, partly because of a monopoly granted to the East India Company which was in place until 1798. Once that was lifted, the sea off the north coast of New Zealand became an increasingly common destination for whaling captains whose hunt for whale oil took them across the globe. And once there, they found the people of Pēwhairangi ready to supply them with a sheltered port of call where they could carry out repairs and gather supplies, including potatoes.

From 1801 the number of ships off the New Zealand coast steadily grew. That year seven ships were recorded in what became known as 'the fishery', including the *Albion*, which had arrived from London with Captain Bunker at the helm. Two years later Bunker and the *Albion* were back, having sailed again from England in the middle of 1802. Like most British whaling ships that visited the fishery, the *Albion* used Port Jackson as a base, and when it arrived there in July 1803 the ship had on board 65 tons of whale oil 'procured mostly off the Eastern Coast of New Zealand'.[3] But it also traversed the triangular route between Port Jackson, New Zealand and Norfolk Island. Three months before arriving at Sydney the *Albion* had been at Norfolk Island, and when it left again in August 1804 after being loaded with fur-seal skins from Bass Strait it made first for Norfolk

Island and then for London. Several days later the *Adonis* arrived
with 1000 barrels of whale oil, having lately called at Norfolk.

Together Norfolk Island and the Bay of Islands became refreshment
stops for whalers working the waters of the South Pacific. By 1805,
according to Philip Gidley King, now promoted to governor, the
supplies available at Norfolk Island had been 'the means of preserving
the lives of many British seamen, and enabling them to return to
England in perfect health, after being almost constantly at sea during
two and sometimes three years, instead of being the scrobutic
and debilitated men returned when their cruizing was confined to
the coast of South America'. But King was equally convinced of the
importance of the Bay:

> [T]he quantity of seeds and other articles I gave the two
> New Zealanders who visited Norfolk Island in 1794,
> and remained there nine months, have turned to a very
> beneficial account, not only for their own advantage, but also
> in supplying the whaling ships very liberally with potatoes
> and other productions derived from what my two visitors,
> whom I conducted to their homes in 1794, took with them.[4]

After the *Alexander* anchored off the Bay in 1803 its captain,
Robert Rhodes, spoke of the reception he and his crew received
'in the highest terms': 'he procured seven or eight tons of very fine
Potatoes, and other refreshments; with much assistance from the
Natives in wooding and watering'.[5] On the same journey the *Alexander*
took on board a young man from Pēwhairangi named Teina, before
sailing for Port Jackson via Norfolk Island with 50 tons of whale oil.
Teina, following in the footsteps of Tuki and Huru, became the first of
the number of Māori to visit Sydney from this point onwards, and the
first to become involved in the whaling industry first-hand.[6]

Two years later, in 1805, Te Pahi sent his son Matara to Sydney
on board the *Ferret* to meet Governor King and to 'see the English

at their settlement'.[7] After staying a month, Matara returned home
on board the *Venus* with gifts of tools for his father from Norfolk
Island, followed by the ill-fated return trip during which Te Pahi
and his four sons were mistreated and threatened by Captain
William Stewart. During his stay Te Pahi complained to King about
the behaviour of some of the whalemen who visited the Bay and the
poor treatment that had been meted out to Māori who had gone on
board visiting ships, which now included himself. Before offering
Te Pahi passage home on board the government ship *Lady Nelson*
in early 1806, King recorded the following:

> As all the whalers and other vessels which have visited Tip-a-he's
> residence have expressed the great convenience, hospitality, and
> assistance they have uniformly received from this worthy chief
> and his people, I told him that I should impress on those who
> might visit him the necessity of their conducting themselves
> and people in a peaceable manner, and to give them articles in
> exchange for their potatoes and what stock he may in future have
> to spare – which the supplies of breeding swine and goats, with
> fowls, &c, sent from Norfolk Island, will soon enable him to do.[8]

Now, only a few months later, the *Venus* was back, and it would be
up to Te Pahi to decide how the mutineers and runaways on board
would be dealt with.

✳ ✳ ✳

The united action that saw some of the crew and passengers seize
control of the *Venus* did not survive the trip across the Tasman Sea.
At some point after it dropped anchor at the Bay of Islands the ship's
human cargo split in two. While Kelly, Hagerty, Lancashire, Badger
and her child – as well as one of the cabin boys, Thomas Ford or
William Evans – got off the *Venus*, the rest of the crew, apparently led

by Joseph Redmonds, kept sailing. What had caused this rupture? The reasons can only be guessed at, but the decision to leave the highest-ranked sailor, Kelly, onshore was a striking repetition of what had happened to Samuel Rodman Chace. If mutineers could turn on a captain once, they could do it again; so had Kelly overstepped his authority among the newly independent crew and been punished for it in a case of 'as the majority gave, so did it take away'?[9] Had the crew found solidarity only in a hatred of Chace and then seen that shared interest fall apart after Chace was gone? Or had Kelly simply been unable to convince the others to stay at the Bay because of the threat of being reported to the Sydney authorities by a visiting whaling captain? And why had Badger, Hagerty and Lancashire joined him? Hagerty, of course, had her own reasons for following Kelly's lead, and Badger might have wanted to stay with the only other woman on board, as well as getting her child to a relatively safe harbour. Lancashire is more of a mystery. Some accounts, such as those in the popular history *The Brown Frontier*, in the Dictionary of New Zealand Biography and in Anne Salmond's *Between Worlds*, have claimed that Badger and Lancashire, like Hagerty and Kelly, formed a shipboard relationship, but there is no direct evidence to support this idea.[10] During the *Venus*'s trip from Port Jackson to Port Dalrymple, Chace made it clear that his first mate had formed an attachment to Hagerty, but he had nothing to say about Badger and Lancashire. Still, it cannot be ruled out, and it would explain Lancashire's decision not to stay with the other single men on board.

Perhaps what truly separated those who stayed on the *Venus* and those who got off, though, was a willingness to live under the protection of Te Pahi. In Louis Becke's version of the *Venus*'s arrival, Kelly invited Māori on board and:

> . . . addressing the leading chiefs, told them that he was
> perfectly well aware of the fact that he and those with him
> were incapable of offering resistance if his visitors attempted

Worcester Guildhall. Photograph by the author.

BLACK-EYED SUE, and SWEET POLL of PLYMOUTH,
Taking leave of their Lovers who are going to Botany Bay.

Publish'd 15 th June 1792 by Rob. Sayer & C.º Fleet Street London.

Robert Sayer, *Black-eyed Sue and Sweet Poll of Plymouth taking leave of their lovers who are going to Botany Bay*, 1792, PIC Drawer 3860 #U5980 NK6972, National Library of Australia. The contemporary idea of idle and dissolute men and women of a criminal class is captured in this satirical print.

Above: John William Lancashire, *View of Sydney Port Jackson, New South Wales,* taken from the Rocks on the western side of the Cove, *c.* 1803, DG SV1 / 60, Dixson Galleries, State Library of New South Wales.

Below: John Heaviside Clark, *A ship's boat attacking a whale; shooting the harpoon,* 1814, PUBL-0005, Alexander Turnbull Library.

A SHIPS BOAT ATTACKING A WHALE.

A contemporary engraving of Mary Read, female pirate and inspiration
for fictional depictions of Badger. Artist unknown.

Top: Augustus Earle, *Tepoanah [Tè Puna] Bay of Islands, New Zealand, a church missionary establishment,* 1827, PIC Solander Box C18 #T176 NK12/139, National Library of Australia. Note that this painting appears to be of the settlement at Wairoa Bay instead of Te Puna Bay.

Bottom: View of Te Puna Bay and Wairoa Bay from Rangihoua pā. Te Puna is in the foreground and Wairoa Bay is in the distance. Photograph by the author.

TIPPAHEE

A

NEW ZEALAND CHIEF

From an Original Drawing by G.P. Harris.

Eng.ᵈ by W. Archibald

George Prideaux Robert Harris, *Tippahee [Te Pahi] a New Zealand
chief / eng[rave]d by W Archibald from an original drawing by G P Harris*, 1827,
A-092-007, Alexander Turnbull Library.

J. Lycett, *West view of Parramatta, 1819*,
FL3140225, Mitchell Library, State
Library of New South Wales.

to cut off the ship. But, he said, he had determined to abandon the ship, and therefore he had invited them on board so that they might take what they wanted from her; and if they had no objection, he and his wife wished to live ashore with them for the future. He then broached a cask of rum. The Maoris appeared to have fallen in with his suggestion with alacrity, and the chief gave the leading mutineer and his wife a large whare to live in, and also gave them two slaves as servants.[11]

Like Becke's portrayal of the riotous life on board the vessel before it was taken, this is an interaction coloured by fanciful invention. But it is also one that, while acknowledging that Māori were the ultimate decision-makers, still cast Kelly as the driving force in the relationship, given the suggestion that Māori 'appeared to have fallen in' line. It is more likely that after arriving at Wairoa Bay, Kelly and the other *Venus* people were required to cross the beach into another world and submit to its rules and controls. The idea of beach crossings belongs to Greg Dening, who saw the beach as a liminal space between worlds, a kind of boundary that had to be passed over, on the other side of which another life and another persona might exist.[12] In the period of early Pacific contact, those people crossing the beach were often drawn from the bottom rungs of European society, most often runaway sailors and ex-convicts. But for those people on the other side of the beach, especially leaders, the new arrivals could play a vital role in interpreting the world of the traders and whaling captains who were coming to their shores. Te Pahi's wish to benefit from the new trading opportunities on offer meant he was willing to make room for people who could act as cultural and linguistic interpreters, but they would have to live by his rules. The people of the *Venus* fitted into this category, but they were not the first, and they were not alone.

Europeans, or Pākehā as their hosts called them, arriving at Wairoa Bay found a home unlike any they had lived in before. A visitor in 1805, John Savage, described the settlement he found, which he incorrectly identified as the neighbouring bay of Te Puna, as follows:

> The capital of this part of the country, which is situated partly on the main land, and partly on a small island, is called Tippoonah [Te Puna], and consists in the whole of about an hundred dwellings. On the main the dwellings of the natives are surrounded each by a little patch of cultivated ground; but the island is appropriated to the residence of a chieftain and his court, where no cultivation is carried on. This island is so exceedingly abrupt in its ascent, and consequently so easily defended against an enemy, that it is frequently the refuge of the natives in time of war. . . . The dwellings of the natives are usually about five feet high, the walls of which are wattled, and made close with rushes. The thatch is of strong bladed grass, and generally well applied. . . .
>
> These are the common lodging-huts of the natives; their cooking operations, which, indeed, do not require a great number of vessels, or attendants, are carried on in a shed at a little distance from the hut, and which is formed by fixing four posts in the ground, about five feet high, on which is laid a flat covering of rushes.

During the same visit in 1805 Savage also recorded the following observation about a runaway convict:

> In many islands of the pacific ocean European fugitives, and others, who have been put on shore for mutinous or improper conduct, have taken up their abode: a man of this description resides in this part of New Zealand: he shuns all communication with Europeans, and on the approach of a ship retires from the coast to the interior. His country, or the motives that induce him to remain here, are unknown: he is

spoken well of by the natives, and has adopted their manners and customs. The native female who associates with him, and one of his children, I have seen several times . . .[13]

This man is often thought to be James Cavanagh, a convict who escaped the government ship the *Lady Nelson* near the Cavalli Islands in June 1804 after it had been forced to seek shelter off the New Zealand coast during a trip in heavy seas from Sydney to Norfolk Island.[14] Two years later the *Lady Nelson* was responsible for bringing yet another runaway to the Bay. When Governor King sent Te Pahi home from his visit to Sydney on that ship in February 1806, one of the seamen working on what would become a two-month slog across the Tasman and down the north-east coast of New Zealand was George Bruce, or Joseph Druce. Bruce had been transported to New South Wales as a child thief and as an adult had been reconvicted and sentenced to six months' hard labour. When he was recaptured following a prison escape, he was allowed to serve time on board government ships. Shortly before the end of the journey, Bruce made a run for it near the Cavalli Islands, just as Cavanagh had before him. He made his way to the Bay of Islands, where Te Pahi 'put him to work as an interpreter and advisor in his dealings with European whalers'.[15] Bruce later claimed that during his two years there he had helped the crews of a number of visiting whalers communicate with local people, including the *Inspector*, *Betsey*, *Governor Bligh*, *Ferret*, *Three Brothers* and *King George*. In late 1807 he helped organise the cutting and loading of spars for Captain Dalrymple of the *General Wellesley*. This vessel had left Port Jackson in April and set out on 'a bricolage of a trading voyage' across the Pacific in search of sandalwood in Fiji, pearls and bêche-de-mer in Tuamotu and, now, timber in New Zealand.[16] It had also stopped at Tahiti for fresh food, where it took on board as pilot Edward Robarts, another runaway sailor who had lived in the Marquesas and who had sometimes acted as a go-between with visiting ships. Robarts had with him his high-born Marquesan wife, Ena, and their two children. In his journal Robarts left behind this impression of George Bruce:

> Bruce came on board. His face being tattowd all over, he might pass for a native. All the people on board that came from Pt Jackson Knew him. Capt D. asked him if he could procure any quantity of spars that would make masts for a ship. He said, yes, he could get the ship loaded. He askd the Capt if he had any iron to make axes. . . . He went up a small river in a canoe and in two or three days returnd for the Boat to tow down the spars.[17]

Like Cavanagh and Robarts, Bruce was an intermediary between worlds, the most obvious marker being the moko etched into his face. And like Robarts his position in his new home had been cemented by marriage to a woman of high birth, in Bruce's case Te Pahi's youngest daughter, Atahoe. By Bruce's own account these two events went hand in hand: 'After I had been amongst them seven months I consented to be marked in the face where I received my wife with all the power that country possessed.'[18] While he was overstating both the element of choice in the matter and his personal power, Bruce's marriage to one of Te Pahi's daughters was a sign of the value he held as an interpreter and cultural mediator. He was also a signifier of Te Pahi's mana, as a chief able to attract and cultivate relationships with traders and the governor of Sydney and the material goods they brought. And playing that role allowed Bruce to achieve a status that escaped him in his own society, where he was viewed as little more than refuse.

These three men, all sailors, were solo emissaries who encountered a new culture by taking their fates into their own hands and escaping the authority that ruled their lives. The same was now true of the *Venus* people, but unlike Cavanagh, Robarts and Bruce, Badger and her companions did not come alone. They would need to be welcomed as a group, and as a group that, for the first time, included women.

Charlotte Badger and Catherine Hagerty were not the first Pākehā women to come to New Zealand and stay. In 1795 Elizabeth Heatherly (also known as Bason) and Anne Carey had been on board the *Endeavour*, a broken-down East India Company vessel not to be confused with James Cook's famous ship, when it had wrecked at Dusky Sound on a seal-hunting expedition before a planned trip to Bengal. The crew built a new ship, *Providence*, out of the remnants, and in early 1796 it sailed to Norfolk Island. Heatherly, like Badger, was accompanied by a small child, and together mother and son became part of the first group of half-starved human flotsam to appeal for Lieutenant-Governor King's mercy upon arrival. Carey, one of a number of escaped convicts who had stolen away on the ill-fated ship, finally made it to Norfolk on a later getaway voyage. Unlike Badger and Hagerty, though, the women of the *Endeavour* were never dependent on Māori, and in fact accounts of the episode make no mention of meeting local people at all.[19] Badger and Hagerty were, as far as we know, the first Pākehā women to experience life on the other side of the beach, in a Māori community, subject to the protection of a rangatira.

One of the sources by which we know that these two women and other *Venus* people were landed at the Bay of Islands comes from Te Pahi's son, the peripatetic Matara. Sometime at the end of September or early October 1806 he once again left the Bay, this time on board the whaler *Richard and Mary*, which was on its way to London. In April 1807 he met Sir Joseph Banks and recounted that when he had left home, six people from the *Venus* were living there: two men, two women and two children. The women were being kept separate and were being protected by tapu at the chiefs' direction.[20]

This raises the question of the women's role and status in the Māori community in which they now lived and the kind of freedom, or otherwise, they might have enjoyed. In her study of the concept of slavery in Māori society, Hazel Petrie made the point that early European arrivals could be treated as captives or slaves if they were 'those whom Māori recognised as people of little status in the Western world', especially convicts.[21] She also made the case, in relation to Māori war captives, that they were 'forced to perform not only the unpleasant work despised by people of higher status, but also that which was most damaging to tapu and mana', although this was not necessarily the case for high-ranking captives. For those of low rank, captivity was a form of humiliation. Therefore, if Badger and Hagerty were indeed being protected by tapu, then this suggests they were viewed as having some value to the chief or chiefs under whose protection they lived, rather than being people of no importance. But Petrie also argues that women could become concubines or wives, especially if they were young, in a similar way as men like George Bruce had been bonded to the community by marriage.[22] It seems possible, then, that Badger and Hagerty filled this role. Certainly, historians who have written about Badger have made similar claims, with James Belich writing that 'Badger lived for some years with a Maori chief', Vincent O'Malley saying, 'It appears she lived for many years as the wife of "one of the inferior chiefs" at the Bay of Islands', and Barbara Brookes claiming that she 'took up with a local Ngāpuhi chief [and raised] a child'.[23] The source of this idea can be traced to evidence given to the Bigge Commission of Inquiry into the government of New South Wales by Ensign Macrae of the *Dromedary*, who, when asked about runaway convicts in New Zealand, stated 'I have only heard of one a woman, who had been there several years, and lived with one of the inferior chiefs.'[24] Macrae did not name the woman or identify where she lived, but the assumption has been made that this was Badger.

Despite the questionable source of the story of Badger's connection to a local rangatira, there are grounds for believing it was possible, given that this was the experience of other women, both in New Zealand and in other Pacific locations, who found themselves dependent on men of power and influence. Only a matter of several years earlier, in 1802, the American ship *Portland* was attacked at Tongatapu. The captain, Lovett Mellen of Massachusetts, was killed along with the mate and most of the crew, although a small group, including an American woman named Elizabeth Morey, her African-American maid and a Hawaiian crew member, were spared. Morey was the first white woman recorded in Tonga. During the two years she spent there she was given the name Lolohea and became absorbed into village life by adopting Tongan dress and becoming the wife of a local leader, Teukava. When in 1804 another American ship, the *Union*, called at Tongatapu on its way to Fiji looking for sandalwood, Morey swam to the ship and warned the crew of a planned attack before being taken on board and given passage to Sydney.

A similar episode happened thirty years later in New Zealand. In 1834 Betty Guard, her whaler husband Jacky and their children were returning to New Zealand from Sydney when their ship, the *Harriet*, encountered a storm off the Taranaki coast and was wrecked. Once ashore they were attacked and captured by a group of Taranaki and Ngāti Ruanui Māori, while some of their shipmates were killed. Jacky was released on the condition that he return with gunpowder as ransom for his wife and children. While he was gone, Betty was initially subjected to violence, although some reports say that she was subsequently well treated and went on to become the wife of a local chief, Oaoiti. Jacky eventually returned with a naval ship, the *Alligator*, and a party of soldiers to rescue his family. After a violent struggle, Betty and her children escaped, although her daughter died only a matter of months after the ordeal.

The stories of Morey and Guard differ from Charlotte Badger's in that Badger did not find herself at the Bay following the violent deaths of her shipmates, and because she landed at a location where the leading rangatira was actively seeking a relationship with Europeans. But there were some significant similarities between the women's experiences, most particularly in that they found themselves living on the other side of the beach following a sudden rupture in a voyage and in the process became reliant on the protection of men of stature. The absence of violence in Badger's story suggests that she experienced less coercion than the other two women; at the same time, she and Hagerty would have had little option but to agree to enter relationships with rangatira on whom their survival now depended. It could be argued that this put them in a situation little different from that which they had left behind in Sydney, where women had few alternatives to reliance on male protectors. But now they were living in an environment where they did not understand the rules of engagement and where every aspect of their lives was determined by their hosts, from the language being spoken to the food being eaten. It is impossible to think that they were unchanged by such an immersive experience, even if we cannot know whether they took to their new lives willingly or with reluctance.

There is reason, though, to believe that whatever their initial motivation for sojourning at Wairoa Bay, dissatisfaction and discomfort soon set in. As Caroline Ralston has pointed out when looking at beachcombers across the Pacific, 'of the hundreds who landed on the islands, few stayed longer than six months; incoming vessels usually found as many men ready to re-embark as there were wanting to leave. Disillusionment with island life was, in fact, rapid among most Europeans.'[25] The *Venus* people's residence at the Bay proved to be temporary, too, although disenchantment has not been put forward as the reason at least two of them left around six months after arriving.

In April 1807, the same month that Matara met with Banks in London, news of the *Venus* and those on board reached Sydney, via two ships. The first was the *Commerce*, which arrived from the subantarctic islands with seal skins for the London market. On the way back to Sydney it had called in at Te Pahi's settlement, 'where captain Birney was given to understand that the *Venus*, which was piratically seized and taken away from Port Dalrymple, had been there, and Kelly left behind with Lancashire; that the former had been taken by the master of the *Britannia*, and went home a prisoner; that the latter had also been made prisoner, and was taken away in the *Brothers*.'[26] In a book on Pākehā captives, Trevor Bentley took this report one step further by suggesting that Kelly and Lancashire were 'enslaved and sold. Lancashire was sold to the captain of the *Brothers* and taken to trial in Sydney. Kelly was sold to the captain of the *Britannia* before being taken to trial in England.'[27] This suggestion borrows from Petrie's argument that convicts could be treated as slaves by Māori communities, but there is no evidence that Te Pahi or any other rangatira sold the two men to passing captains. At the same time, a desire to stay onside with the authorities in Sydney might have prevented them from doing anything to stand in the captains' way.

And what of Badger and Hagerty? The very same day the *Commerce* docked in Sydney, the *Elizabeth*, under the command of Kelly's former captain Eber Bunker, also arrived at the end of a whaling trip to New Zealand waters. The *Sydney Gazette* reported that the previous December the *Elizabeth* had encountered the *Indispensible* north of New Zealand. The master of that ship, Captain Turnbull, said he had been at the Bay and told Bunker that 'two women and a child were put on shore with Kelly and Lancashire, together with some stores, and that the charge of the vessel had then fallen to a black man [Redmonds], who had avowed an inclination of returning to Port Jackson, but was incapable of piloting her to any determinate place whatever'. Bunker then went to the Bay himself, where he found that 'one of the women [had] died on shore there; the other, with her child, captain Bunker offered to take on board, but she declined the proffer'.[28]

According to this version of events, then, by early in 1807 Badger and her child were the only people from the *Venus* left at the Bay, with the fate of the cabin boy mentioned by Matara remaining unexplained. But how much of it is true, or at least how much of it can be judged to be possible? We know that Matara confirmed that six people from the *Venus* were living at the Bay, but what can we say about the stories of Kelly and Lancashire being taken away on the *Britannia* and the *Brothers*, or of Bunker speaking to Badger? Also, if Bunker encountered Badger, why did she avoid the attention of Captain Birnie of the *Commerce* during its visit, given that he did not mention seeing her?

At the heart of this mystery are five vessels, the *Brothers*, the *Indispensible*, the *Elizabeth*, the *Britannia* and the *Commerce*, that navigated the waters between New South Wales, Norfolk Island and New Zealand over an eight-month period between August 1806 and April 1807. Each of these ships is a piece in a puzzle that, when laid out, can be fitted together to explain what might have happened to those on board the *Venus*. What follows is a reconstruction of events that takes the reports in the *Sydney Gazette* and matches them against the movement of the ships to see if those reports were in any way plausible.

The first vessel, the *Britannia*, had arrived in Sydney in June 1806 from the California coast, having left England twenty-two months earlier.[29] By September, it was setting sail for London with a full load of whale oil; it completed its long journey by arriving there in April 1807. A speculative trip to New Zealand waters before finally heading for London would have allowed the ship to collect Kelly in October 1806 after he had been seen at the Bay by Matara. These types of final visits were not uncommon and had been undertaken by both the *Richard and Mary* in 1806 and the HMS *Reliance* in 1800.

The *Britannia*'s departure from Sydney came a month after the *Brothers*, an American whaler registered in Nantucket that had been operating out of Sydney since 1805, which left Sydney in mid-August. In November it was seen north of Sydney by the *Argo*. At the time the *Brothers*'s master, Captain Worth, reported he was heading for Norfolk Island, 'and from thence for the Coast of New Zealand to complete his cargo, having already about 1000 barrels; and will then quit the fishery.'[30] Worth was as good as his word, as this was the last time the *Brothers* was recorded in New Zealand or Australian waters. A last trip to the Bay in late November or early December could have seen Captain Worth taking Lancashire on board, after Kelly.

By December, the *Indispensible*, which had left England in May, was off the northern coast of New Zealand, where its master, Captain Turnbull, and Bunker took part in a whalers' gam, or conversation at sea, wherein Turnbull reported that he had recently been at the Bay of Islands.[31] By the time Turnbull arrived both Kelly and Lancashire could have been taken away, leaving the two women behind.

The *Indispensible* was followed by the *Elizabeth*, which had left Sydney in September and arrived back at that port in April.[32] When Bunker got to the Bay, possibly in January or February 1807, he found the two men gone and Badger alone, following the death of her female companion, Hagerty perhaps having died in the interim between the *Indispensible*'s visit and his own.

Finally, the *Commerce* left Sydney in February 1807, with the man in charge, Captain Birnie, claiming he was heading for England. The vessel was back in April, though, after a surreptitious trip to the Penantipodes and a stopover at the Bay of Islands.[33] Arriving after the previous four vessels, and after Kelly's and Lancashire's removal and Hagerty's death, Birnie encountered none of the *Venus* people and reported only their absence.

This reconstruction offers a way of making sense of the reports of the *Venus*'s passengers but it does not explain why Birnie did not see Charlotte Badger when he visited the Bay. To understand the answer to this question we do not have to rely on speculation. Instead, thanks to the scrupulous record-keeping of colonial officials we know that she was gone before Birnie arrived. In early 1807 the *Indispensible* was back at the Bay, at which point it collected Badger and took her to Norfolk Island; by the middle of June she was on board the government ship *Porpoise* on her way back to Sydney. The passenger list for that voyage recorded the following: 'Charlotte Badger Brought from New Zealand on the Indispensible and is one of the women on the Venus schooner when run away with from P. Dalrymple.'[34] Like Te Pahi and Elizabeth Heatherly before her, Badger's journey away from New Zealand used Norfolk Island as a first port of call and a stepping stone on a longer voyage. The reason for her decision to leave cannot be known, but being the only one of her shipmates left onshore must have acted as a powerful motivation to return to her former, more familiar, life, even if it meant taking her chances with the authorities.

This, then, was Badger's fate: as a woman at the end of a year-long journey of escape to a new and strange land, without her companions, and it seems without her child also, on her way back to the place that had been her home for five of the past six years. Paradoxically, for someone whose life has been the subject of so much supposition, she is the only person who travelled on the *Venus* whose destiny can be known, and it was one marked by the scattering of her companions and probable grief for a lost child.

But this long, lonely trip home is not the story that has been told about Badger. Instead, her life has been given a different outcome altogether, on the other side of the globe, because the record of her trip to Norfolk Island and then to Sydney has lain in an archive and in its absence other stories have been told and retold. Although two of the earliest accounts of the *Venus*, in Sherrin and Wallace's *Early History of New Zealand* (1890) and in *From Tasman to Marsden* by Robert McNab, published in 1914, made no comment about her ultimate fate, and Jack Lee in his 1983 book on the Bay of Islands said that nothing was known on the subject, other more recent histories have taken imaginary leaps and offered a vision of her as a traveller across oceans.[35] Again, the Dictionary of New Zealand Biography, while acknowledging the uncertain direction of her life, nonetheless offered some possibilities:

On two occasions she was offered a passage back to Port
Jackson. She refused, and in 1808 said she would prefer to die
among the Māori. . . . Charlotte Badger's fate is not known.
. . . About 1826 a ship which had visited Tonga reported
that an English woman with a girl of about eight years had
landed there 10 years previously. The woman had said she was
escaping from the Maori of New Zealand. Her description,
'A very big stout woman', fitted Charlotte Badger. . . . One
account of her life claims that she finally escaped to America,
and the ship may have called at Tonga on the journey across
the Pacific.[36]

The story of Badger travelling to Tonga is also found in popular
histories *Coasts of Treachery* and *The Brown Frontier*, published two
decades earlier, in 1963 and 1967 respectively. It has also been
offered by historians, including Anne Salmond, who wrote that
'apparently [Badger] and her daughter eventually made their way
to Tonga – not bad for an ex-housebreaker', as well as Vincent
O'Malley, who has Badger 'popping up in the historical record in
Tonga in 1818'.[37] These stories can be traced to Louis Becke, the
weaver of fact and fiction who had spun Badger as the piratical leader
into being. In 1895 Becke recounted how in 1826 an American ship,
the *La Fayette*, called at a small Tongan island. The captain, through
an interpreter, was told that his ship was only the second such vessel
to come to the island, the first one having arrived around ten years
earlier. On board that earlier ship was a woman who had apparently
'escaped captivity with the Maoris'. She was also described as having
a daughter of around eight years old, and as being 'a very big, stout
woman'. The presence of the daughter, along with the similarity
of the woman's physical appearance to that contained in the *Sydney
Gazette* public notice, which had noted that Badger was 'very
corpulent', led Becke to assert that 'No doubt this was the woman
Badger'.[38] And once again, Becke's account was taken up by the

writer of Badger's story in the *Sydney Morning Herald* in 1937, who expanded and embellished even further:

> In 1826, twenty years after the Venus had cleared Sydney Heads, the American ship Lafayette called at Vavau, in the Tongan Islands, during a voyage to Sydney.
>
> On her arrival in Sydney, the Lafayette brought the last news of the Indomitable Badger. It appeared that, in 1818 an American whaler had called at Vavau on her homeward voyage, and on board was a woman who must have been our own pirate lady.
>
> Speaking a Polynesian dialect fluently – as well she might after living with Maoris for twelve years – Charlotte had related her experiences in New Zealand to the Tongans. They described her as being an enormously fat woman with a young child – poor Charlotte had evidently lost her looks after feasting all those years in Maori villages.
>
> When an American ship had finally called near her settlement Charlotte had either wished to die among her own race, or else had formed a middle-aged attachment with the American whaling skipper.[39]

It is a testament to the global reach of the trading networks criss-crossing the Pacific in the early nineteenth century that these versions of events are at least plausible. Even as British administrators, army officers, convicts, traders and whalers were travelling to and building Sydney from the ground up, they were joined on the open ocean by American captains and their motley crews, who traced their home bases to New England. And as Sydney's traders and American captains headed into New Zealand waters, those islands became a destination on a global highway.

Before there was a United States, Americans were venturing out across the Atlantic and, later, the Pacific in search of whales, first of the right and then of the sperm variety. The earliest ventures were launched from the island of Nantucket, a tiny strip of crescent-shaped land barely staving off the sea that surrounds and threatens to drown it. By the middle of the eighteenth century 150 whalers were operating from the island. By that time, it had been joined by another Massachusetts locality, New Bedford, as a launching pad for voyages across the world in search of the oil that powered lamps and candles, as well as seal skins. Then, when the crisis of the American Revolution struck, ship owners such as Enderby and Sons went into business with British firms and lured American whalemen across the Atlantic to London in order to stay afloat, while others toughed it out at home. After the war, untroubled by the limits placed on British traders by the East India Company monopoly, the American moves into the Pacific gained pace. In the years that followed, American captains went into business with Sydney traders like Simeon Lord against the express orders of the administrators who tried unsuccessfully to maintain British control over the trade in Australasian waters.

Two Americans, both Massachusetts men, who lived through the aftermath of the crisis of war played roles in the *Venus* drama. The first was Benjamin Worth, captain of the *Brothers*. A Nantucketer, Worth had taken to the sea at the age of fifteen and stayed there almost continuously for the next half-century, returning home only between the end of one whaling voyage and the start of the next. During that time, he estimated he had sailed '879,960 miles and circumnavigated the world twice, rounding Cape Horn sixteen times and the Cape of Good Hope twice. He had visited over forty island groups in the Pacific and Atlantic oceans, some of them many times, and traversed the entire west coast of South America and as far as the Columbia River on the northwest American coast.'[40]

The second was Eber Bunker, the man who had apparently encountered Badger first-hand. Bunker was a Nantucket name, but Eber Bunker did not hail from there. Instead, he was from Plymouth, although unlike Worth he had followed Nantucketers when they left New England for old England in the wake of war in order to save his economic fortunes.[41] From there he had sailed the *William and Ann* to Port Jackson and then brought the ship to New Zealand waters in 1792, followed later by other vessels, including the *Albion* and the *Elizabeth*.[42] His voyages took him across the Pacific to Tahiti, New Caledonia and Tongatapu, as well as to Bengal, before he left the sea and settled land in New South Wales.

Bunker's travels to Tonga were part of the irregular but not uncommon trips to the so-called Friendly Islands by both American and British ships in search of sandalwood, whales, food and water. Contrary to the name James Cook had given to Tonga, that destination, along with Fiji, gained a ferocious reputation in Sydney because of the violence that often accompanied crews' efforts to harvest natural resources. In 1809, for example, the *Mercury* put in at Vava'u for water, where a European beachcomber named Blake warned the captain not to trade for fear that the vessel would be attacked. Blake had been there for several years, having been on board the *Port au Prince* when it was set upon at Ha'apai in 1806. The captain and almost all the crew were killed, but a handful of men had escaped and had scattered across the island group. Blake claimed that the attack had been assisted by a Hawaiian, one of a number of crew members from those islands who had been on board. Interestingly, in Becke's account of the *La Fayette*'s visit to Tonga in 1826, it was a Hawaiian from the *Port au Prince* who acted as interpreter and told that vessel's captain about his encounter with the woman Becke identified as Charlotte Badger.

A similar fate had befallen the American ship *Portland* that carried Elizabeth Morey. It is perhaps more than a coincidence that she, too, was a subject of Louis Becke's writing. When she reached Sydney, Morey became the subject of coverage in the *Sydney Gazette*; ninety-seven years later that reporting formed the basis of Becke's story 'The Adventure of Elizabeth Morey of New York'.[43] When Becke wrote of Charlotte Badger's fate it bore elements of Morey's story, in that she was in Tonga on board an American ship while escaping a hostile host. The potential that Becke was constructing a fictional account that combined the two women's experience is reinforced by the likelihood that the *La Fayette* was a figment of his imagination, given that no such vessel can be found in any shipping registers or reports of the time. There is the compounding difficulty that the ship was supposed to be from Salem, Massachusetts, a port whose role as an international entrepôt was over by 1820 and didn't revive until 1831 when its whaling industry was resurrected.[44] Becke took the trouble to insert elements of believability in his account of Badger's trip via Tonga, including the Hawaiian interpreter from the *Port au Prince*, but the trip itself never took place.

If we can come to some settled conclusions about what happened to Badger, what can we say about the fates of her companions Kelly and Lancashire? Here, we have only speculation to fill the gaps. There are no comparable records of what happened to the two men. While the movements of the *Brothers* and the *Britannia* mean that they may very well have left the Bay on those ships, their ultimate destinations remain a mystery. The story offered in the *Sydney Gazette* has the *Brothers* returning Lancashire to New South Wales to face trial, but the ship did not return to Port Jackson after its final trip to New Zealand waters and no record of Lancashire in New South Wales exists after he left on board the *Venus* in 1806. The *Brothers* returned to its home port of Nantucket, possibly via Calcutta. Again, though, no records can be found of him in either of those places. The journey across the globe to New England provided plenty of opportunity for jumping ship or otherwise disappearing, and as far as history is concerned that is exactly what John William Lancashire did.

Likewise, Benjamin Kelly was described in the *Sydney Gazette* as being taken to England on the *Britannia* to face justice, but no such justice was meted out. Kelly's fate is the subject of more stories than one, though, with the second being more detailed and far more curious. And it is a supposed destiny that is inextricably tied up with the fate of the *Venus* itself.

The accepted version of the last days of the *Venus* is based in part on the word of Samuel Marsden, recorded during his trip down the east coast of the North Island on board the *Active* in 1815, following his arrival at Rangihoua just before Christmas the previous year. According to his account, the stolen ship called in at various points along the coast, taking away local women at each anchorage. At Bream Head he recounted:

> We enquired if any vessel had ever been in this harbour. The natives told us that the Venus, from Port Jackson, a long time ago anchored there some time. They further informed us that the Venus had put in at the North Cape and took two native women from there, one from the Bay of Islands, one from a small island opposite to Bream Cove, and one from Bream Cove, and from thence she went to the river Thames [Waihou] where they got Houpa and one of his daughters on board with an intention to take them away also. When the Venus sailed from the river Thames, Houpa's canoe following the Venus, he watched an opportunity and leaped overboard and was taken up by his canoe, but that none of the above women have ever since returned.[45]

The details of the *Venus*'s rapacious visit to the Waihou River were also reported by John Liddiard Nicholas, who was travelling on the *Active* with Marsden:

> This river has, I believe, been very little visited by Europeans. Captain Cook was the first that ever entered it, which he did in his first voyage in the year 1769. Besides his vessel, and the one I have just noticed, the Royal Admiral, I could discover but only two others that anchored here: the Venus, a small

brig carried off by the convicts from the river Derwent in
Van Dieman's Land, and the Fanny, an inconsiderable vessel,
commanded by Captain Dell, who cut down three thousand
spars as a cargo for a transport ship that was to call for them on
her return from Port Jackson. The convicts, in their predatory
descents upon the surrounding country, had the barbarity to
carry off with them the daughter of Shoupah [Houpa], and
would have likewise taken away the chief himself, had he not
made his escape from the unfeeling wretches.[46]

Neither Marsden nor Nicholas provided any clue to the *Venus*'s
ultimate fate, though. Speculation on that point was left to Robert
McNab, who in his book *From Tasman to Marsden* repeated an
untraceable assertion that 'the colonial schooner *Mercury*, which
touched at New Zealand, learned that she [*Venus*] had been taken
by the Natives, who killed and ate her crew and burnt the hull for
the sake of the iron'.[47] This story, with its almost predictable and
unproven claim of Māori savagery, echoed an assertion made in
the *Sydney Gazette* at the time the *Commerce* returned to Sydney
and reported the crew's misfortune, which held that 'the vessel is
supposed to be still wandering the coast, as she had no navigator
on board; and no passable prospect can present itself to those that
remain in her, but to perish by the hands of the natives, or to fall
into the hands of justice'.[48] McNab's story is contradicted, however,
by an 1808 report, also in the *Sydney Gazette*, stating that 'the Venus,
taken from Port Dalrymple, with every requisite on board, was last
seen upon the coast of New Zealand, in a distressed condition, and
has never since been heard of'.[49] After two years, Sydney still had
no idea what had become of the pirate ship.

Like other elements of the Badger story, this confusion gave rise
to fantastical possibilities, the most colourful of which involved a
sighting in South America. In *The Brown Frontier*, C. W. Vennell
presented a version of the *Venus*'s fate that saw the vessel initially carry

on down the New Zealand coast under Redmonds's command, but then turn around, return to the Bay, collect Kelly and island-hop across the Pacific to Chile. Along the way it jettisoned what remained of its original crew and collected 'runaway sailors or escaped convicts who had drifted to the remote islands of the South Pacific'.[50] In January 1807 it was sighted 'close inshore from the small Spanish–American town of Carampangue', before heading away to the port of Concepción. Once there, according to Vennell, Benjamin Kelly identified both himself and his ship to local authorities, saying 'they had come all the way from Port Jackson, the main British convict settlement in New South Wales, 8,000 miles away on the other side of the Pacific'. By this time the *Venus* was flying an American flag, to distinguish itself from a British ship following the outbreak of war with Spain in 1804, but Kelly was still subjected to an official investigation. Kelly apparently spun a tale that Vennell labels a fantasy masquerading as an alibi which had him first entering the Pacific as first mate on a sealing ship called the *Pelican*. This vessel eventually made its way to Port Jackson. There, the captain bought the *Venus*, which then sailed under Kelly's command via New Zealand, where they collected a Māori crew, including women. After giving this account of his movements he was able to convince his interrogators he was an American citizen, and following the sale of the *Venus* he made his way to Lima and from there to New York.

Vennell's source was an article written in 1955 by Eugenio Pereira Salas about early contacts between Australia and Chile.[51] Unfortunately for Vennell, Salas's version of events was somewhat less compelling than he suggests. Salas's account does involve a ship named the *Venus* under the command of Captain Kelly making landfall in Chile in January 1807. And Kelly does tell investigators a story about going on a Pacific sealing trip on board the *Pelican* and then buying the *Venus* at 'New Holland'. But Captain Kelly is not identified as Benjamin Kelly and there is no mention of New Zealand. Vennell was right that the *Pelican* story is problematic in that no ship by that name can be found entering Port Jackson; then again, Captain Kelly never explicitly says that the *Venus* was bought at that port. But Vennell's conclusions are laden with even more problems because of the assumptions and leaps of logic and imagination involved. There is simply no evidence to suggest that the vessel that was pirated at Port Dalrymple returned to the Bay, picked up Benjamin Kelly and crossed the Pacific. A Captain Kelly may very well have sailed to Concepción and then travelled onwards to New York, but the evidence that he was Benjamin Kelly, shipmate of Charlotte Badger, does not exist. Despite this, Ian Duffield, in his account of the *Venus*, took Vennell's interpretation of Salas's evidence at face value and repeated this new outcome without apparently questioning it further.[52]

Kelly's ultimate fate, like Lancashire's and even Hagerty's is, like the ship they travelled on, unknown. We simply don't know whether or where the *Venus* wrecked, or what became of the remainder of the crew who sailed it away from the Bay. And we cannot trace Badger's companions as they jumped ship, made their way to a new home or died in the process of getting there. But as they scattered to the wind, Charlotte Badger was on a boat back to New South Wales to meet whatever destiny awaited her at the penal colony she had escaped only a year before.

The
Army Wife

On 12 June 1807 a rowboat made its way across the water towards the HMS *Porpoise*, moored off the coast of Norfolk Island. On board was Charlotte Badger, on the final leg of a trip that had taken her on the triangular route to Van Diemen's Land, the Bay of Islands and now Norfolk. She had been on the island for several months after arriving on board the *Indispensible*, living on government stores. Now the government was sending her on the final leg of her journey, back to Sydney. After several weeks on a rough sea, she arrived back in Port Jackson to begin her old life anew.

Thanks to the bureaucratic requirements imposed on colonial officials, we know how the government viewed Badger. The *Porpoise*'s passenger list, which described her as 'one of the women on the Venus schooner when run away with from P. Dalrymple', strongly implies that officials saw her as a passive actor in the piracy of the *Venus*, as a woman caught up in events beyond her control instead of a transgressor in her own right.[1] The fact that the government did not take any action against her once she was back in Sydney seems to confirm this view. Instead of being prosecuted as a runaway, she was allowed to merge back into Sydney society and resume her life.

The lack of interest in her return is notable in another way, too. She was a woman who, as far as the government was concerned, had been taken by pirates and who had spent months living among strange people in a strange land, and yet the local press paid her no attention. This apparent indifference was in stark contrast to the way they had treated the tale of Elizabeth Morey when she was brought to Sydney in 1804 following her escape from Tongatapu. Morey had become a focus of press coverage when she retold her story as part of an investigation into the attacks on the *Portland* and the *Union*, the ship that had brought her to the Pacific and the vessel that had transported her to Sydney. Badger's arrival back as a sole emissary and the lack of any public enquiry allowed her to slip quietly into obscurity and her fate to go unnoticed by the public.

What's more, at the time of her return the colony had other things on its mind. Badger had been brought back to Sydney by Lieutenant John Putland, a navy man who had served under Horatio Nelson before coming to New South Wales in early August 1806 in the company of the colony's new governor, his father-in-law William Bligh. Putland had travelled on board the *Porpoise* under the command of Joseph Short, but Bligh put him in charge of the vessel once it reached Port Jackson owing to ongoing tension between Short and the new man in charge. By the beginning of 1808 Putland was dead from tuberculosis, which at least spared him the pain of watching what came next, as Bligh's governorship came to a crashing, humiliating end.

Within a month of Putland's death, the officers of the New South Wales Corps rose up in what became known as the Rum Rebellion, overthrowing Bligh and placing both him and his daughter, Mary, under house arrest. The roots of Bligh's downfall lay in his ability to antagonise almost every sector of Sydney society, including local traders and prominent leaseholders, as well as in his own irascibility and rigid dedication to the strictures of government. He had arrived at a time when the colony was again short of food, following devasting floods along the Hawkesbury River, and his sympathies, not unreasonably, lay with those smallholders who had suffered losses. He set about diverting the colony's stores and other resources to help them, which disturbed the balance of the local economy. In the process, he earned the gratitude of farmers while provoking the hostility of emancipist traders. He further upset the standing economic order when he tried to break the hold the officers in the New South Wales Corps had over the rum trade. Wealthy landowners like Simeon Lord were forbidden to build on their own land, while those further down the pecking order, too, felt the force of Bligh's reforming zeal when he ordered householders occupying the Domain to be removed and their houses pulled down. Perhaps his biggest mistake, though, was taking legal proceedings against a former officer in the Corps turned leaseholder, John Macarthur. When Macarthur failed to abide by a court order, he was arrested and required to attend trial, which he also failed to do. Six of the men who made up the court were officers of the New South Wales Corps, while the seventh was Richard Atkins, Catherine Hagerty's former employer and known enemy of Macarthur. Macarthur's protest that Atkins was biased against him had the support of the other six men, whom Bligh then accused of treasonous behaviour. When Bligh called on the officer in charge of the Corps, Major Johnston, to deal with his men, he responded by arresting Bligh instead and removing him from power. Bligh finally left the colony two years later.

Bligh was not the first governor to get on the wrong side of the New South Wales Corps, but he was the only one to succumb so totally to its power. The Corps had first arrived in the colony in 1790, following the removal of the marines who had accompanied Arthur Phillip. When Phillip left in 1792, it was almost three years before the next governor, Hunter, arrived, and during that time the

Corps effectively took hold of the government. The officers took the opportunity to acquire land and a monopoly in the rum trade, which they imported from India and then used to barter for goods such as grain, at great profit to themselves. It was this trade that earned them the name the 'Rum Corps'. Both governors Hunter and King tried to break the power of the Corps, to little avail. In the end, it was their action against Bligh that saw them brought to heel, when in 1809 Bligh's successor, Lachlan Macquarie, brought his own regiment, the 73rd, to replace them, and most of their number returned to England.

Some of the Corps, though, stayed in New South Wales. These men, numbering around three hundred, had been in the colony for years and had formed attachments, including wives and children. None of them were young, and they would have been subject to discharge if they returned to England, although they were still capable of carrying out garrison duty. Macquarie sought permission to form them into a Veterans, or Invalids, Company for this purpose, which was granted in 1810.[2] One of these men was named Thomas Humphries, and a year later, in 1811, he married Charlotte Badger.[3]

The wedding took place on 4 June at St Philip's church in Sydney, described as 'the ugliest church in Christendom'.[4] The church register records the bride as Charlotte Badgery and the groom as 'Thomas Humphries Private Invalids of this place'; neither of them signed their name but left an X instead. She was aged thirty-three; he was forty-eight. There to act as witnesses were John and Sarah Hefferon.[5] A couple by that name had married in the same church on the same day exactly one year earlier, the bride's name being Sarah Priestly. The Veterans Company contained a private called John Hefferon, from Galway, while a woman named Sarah Priestly had been convicted at Colchester in July 1800 and arrived in Sydney on board the *Nile* in December 1801, six months after Badger. She had been married to Joseph Priestly at the time she was transported, but it is not known if he was still alive when she married Hefferon. It seems probable, then, that the couples shared the bond of being a soldier husband and an ex-convict wife.

Thomas Humphries was a veteran of the British Army in the truest sense; by the time he and Charlotte Badger married he had been enlisted for over twenty years. Born in Bury St Edmunds, in Suffolk, he had joined the 60th Regiment of Foot in 1787, aged twenty-four. Then, after three years' service, he left in 1790, before re-enlisting in 1792. This time he stayed. He was assigned to the 45th Regiment of Foot and then the 87th Regiment of Foot and spent six years in the West Indies protecting British interests against the French and somehow surviving the illnesses that claimed horrifying numbers of his fellow soldiers. Around 40,000 British soldiers died in the West Indies between 1793 and 1798 alone, most of whom succumbed to disease.[6] By 1806, now in his forties, Private Humphries was part of the detachment of the 2nd Royal Veteran Battalion that was sent to join the New South Wales Corps, meaning he was a member of that outfit when its leaders overthrew Bligh. When the 102nd Regiment, as the Corps was known from 1808, returned to Britain in 1810, the man described in his army records as being about 5 foot 5 inches in height, with dark brown hair, blue eyes and a dark complexion, decided to stay in the place that had been his home for only four years.[7]

Thomas Humphries's decision to marry late in life was not unusual. The posting of young men to far-off places made sustaining a marriage difficult, and the army fostered a culture that viewed womanising as a sign of masculinity.[8] What's more, the army actively discouraged marriage by limiting the number of women who could accompany their husbands on active service; regiments dispatched to New South Wales were allowed only twelve wives per company.[9] But these official efforts were not always successful, especially as men got older and the pull of domesticity grew stronger. As Jennine Hurl-Eamon put it, 'Wandering warriors who enjoyed a libertine youth might have grown jaded with these superficial pleasures and dreamt of something more substantial.'[10] The draw of the settled life for older men seems to have been recognised by the army itself, given that veterans battalions were not subjected to the same restrictions on wives that were imposed on other units.[11] But they could still face hostility from outside the army as well as inside. While soldiers suffered from a reputation for loose sexual behaviour and drunkenness, the women who associated with them were often viewed as little more than prostitutes. In New South Wales, this low regard was often exacerbated by women's status as convicts, which as we saw in chapter 2 (The Convict) marked them as immoral harpies. Macquarie echoed these views when he declared himself to be 'against the Military forming Matrimonial, or less proper Connexions with the Women of the Country, whereby they lose sight of their Military duty and become in a great degree identified with the lowest Class of the Inhabitants'.[12] The paradox was that marriage was also supposed to be an indicator of respectability, and a soldier's decision to marry was surely a sign that he wanted a settled, mature life.

For Charlotte Badger, marriage was also a pathway to a new kind of stability. In contrast to the previous decade and a half of her life, which had been characterised by moving from one distant location to another, she would spend the rest of her life in the area north and west of Sydney. That more settled life brought with it another chance at motherhood as well. On Christmas Day 1811, a woman by the name of Charlotte Humphries took part in a churching ceremony in St Philip's, a ritual that involved blessing mothers around six weeks after childbirth. Almost twelve months later, on 15 November 1812, she took part in another.[13] It is likely that only one of these babies survived because in 1814 Badger was listed in the general population muster as having one child. Subsequent records named her as a girl, Maria. Together, Badger and her daughter now followed Humphries to his various postings. She was still subject to rules and regulations, and the rhythm of her life was still dictated by the government, but now that rhythm would be determined by her role as an army wife and mother instead of as a convict. And the army would place her on a new type of frontier, one shaped by conflict and colonial expansion, as well as negotiation.

The men of the Veterans Company were charged with carrying out garrison duty in the out-settlements of Parramatta, Windsor, Liverpool and, later, Emu Plains, as well as other smaller outposts. This non-combat role reflected their age and was in keeping with the part played by veterans battalions in the army generally, which typically involved working in depots and carrying out administrative roles, freeing up the more able-bodied to do the fighting.[14] From the start, though, they were looked down on by those responsible for the colony's defence. In his capacity as Lieutenant-Colonel of the New South Wales Corps, William Paterson described the Veterans in 1807 as 'Old Men . . . who are totally unfit for duty in this Colony'.[15] Still, they would spend the next decade carrying out the duties for which military authorities thought they were unsuited.

Nothing is known of where Thomas and Charlotte spent the first three years of their married life; the Veterans Company muster rolls record only that he was 'on duty'. But from 1814 until 1820 he was stationed at Parramatta, up the river to Sydney's west. The settlement that had briefly been known as Rose Hill had been established in 1788 after Governor Philip's search for fertile land suitable for cropping. Unlike the unruly town at Sydney Cove, Parramatta was to be a planned undertaking, with a broad main street leading up from the water's edge to the governor's new residence. Huts for convicts were to be set out in straight rows, each with its own garden.[16] In 1794 a soldier recorded his impressions of a verdant, almost idyllic locale:

> Paramatta is a town situated at the extreme cove of Port Jackson.
> On your ascending the wharf appears a row of huts on each
> side, and a spacious road to the distance of a mile; at the upper

end, Governor Phillips erected his country seat. The garden
that surrounds it is beautiful, abounding, in the season, with
grapes, melons, pumpkins, and every other fruit and vegetable.
The florist may also amuse himself. In short, the country may
well be called Botany Bay; for the botanist, I believe, may here
find the most beautiful shrubs and evergreens that produce
very fragrant flowers. The Governor's garden at Paramatta is
so situated by nature that, in my opinion, it is impossible for
art to form so rural a scene.[17]

By 1811 a road had been built from Sydney to Parramatta, and a
decade later Governor Macquarie had applied his mania for municipal
order and civic improvement to the town by requiring that anyone
wanting to erect a dwelling or other building submit plans for
approval.[18] He had also added significantly to Parramatta's public
buildings by overseeing the construction of a series of large brick
edifices, including a female orphanage, a hospital, the convict
barracks, a military barracks and the new female factory. The last
of these was the structure designed and built by Francis Greenway
in 1821 that would house the incorrigible women of the worst sort,
the female convicts who had their heads shaved and rioted over food
shortages. Badger was by then a free woman, listed as being 'free by
servitude' in census records. This building and its inhabitants must
have acted as a constant reminder of her former status and as a sign
of the life she had left behind, and it must have given her a way of
measuring the difference between herself as an army wife and the
convicts who were being subjected to Macquarie's increasingly
institutionalised vision of punishment and reform.

In some ways, though, those differences might not have been
all that marked. While it is possible that she and Humphries had
a home of their own in the town and therefore enjoyed private
domesticity, it is also possible that they, like other military couples
and families across the world, lived in British Army barracks. In these

cases, 'Military couples would live with their children in the same overcrowded barrack room with the unmarried soldiers', with the women doing the laundry, cooking, cleaning and sewing for the soldiers. The domestic role that they would normally perform in their own homes was, in this case, carried out in a communal space, and it was a space that was subject to the regulation of the army. Women could, for example, have their rations withdrawn if they did not meet expectations. 'Their "private" married life would happen under the gaze of all the other soldiers and military families living in the same space. At most, they would have a curtain for intimacy.'[19] What's more, living in these conditions and adhering to the army's regulation of soldiers' living arrangements made army wives more likely to be tarred with the brush of immorality, living as they were among a wider company of men. It was a trap not of their own making, but it reinforced preconceptions of them as women of a low moral class.[20]

Along with the government, the church of Samuel Marsden had its own institutions at Parramatta, most obviously St John's Church. And when she looked in that direction, Badger would have seen that another part of her life had followed her to Parramatta, as Māori came there to attend Marsden's purpose-built school. The Māori presence was not a new thing, though. Te Pahi had visited Marsden at Parramatta during his trip to Sydney in 1805, and he was followed by other Bay of Islands leaders, including his kinsman Ruatara, who had left Oihi in 1806 to go whaling and had met Marsden on board the convict ship *Ann* in 1809 when they were both travelling to Sydney from London. The young rangatira had been unwell on the voyage, and Marsden had cared for him. Ruatara went on to live with the Marsden family for two years and establish his own farm at Parramatta, before returning home in 1812. This relationship, formed at sea and cemented at Parramatta, led to the foundation of the Church Missionary Society mission at Rangihoua Bay in 1814, when Ruatara invited Pākehā teachers to come. He travelled to Parramatta to accompany Marsden and his missionaries to New Zealand, along with other leading men Hongi Hika and Korokoro. In turn, this first exercise in permanent Pākehā settlement in New Zealand also led to the setting up of a school 'for the instruction of New Zealanders [Māori]' at Parramatta in 1815. When Marsden returned from establishing the Rangihoua mission station he was accompanied by twelve young male students, the sons of rangatira keen to gain knowledge of the European world and to form alliances with the men of influence in New South Wales.[21] By 1819 this number had grown to sixteen; by the next year it stood at twenty-five, and a dwelling had been erected to house the attendees. This building was known as Rangihou, or Rangihu, and the street on which it was located became New Zealand Street, a slice of the Bay of Islands in New South Wales.[22] By 1822, though, thirteen students had died. The following year Marsden decided to close the school, although it took until 1827 for this to finally happen. The small number of students who remained transferred to the Native Institution, originally set up by Macquarie in 1815 for the education of Aboriginal children, but the fatalities continued, including a young girl named 'Kooley'.

These two establishments, the New Zealand Seminary and the Native Institution, sitting alongside each other in Parramatta, one founded by Marsden's church and the other by Macquarie's state, became living symbols of two frontiers, where two native peoples met the European world. For Charlotte Badger, they would have been reminders of the two borderlands on which she lived, one in the past and one in the present; places where her life intersected with cultures other than her own.

We do not know how she judged those cultures or how she compared their members with each other. We do not know if she shared the ideas of contemporaries such as Marsden, who encountered both Māori and Aboriginal people and who applied prevailing racial attitudes to them, being sure that apparently nomadic Aboriginal people were beyond the reach of 'civilisation', while Māori, who to the European eye displayed recognisable social structures and settlement, were 'a very superior people in point of mental capacity, requiring but the introduction of Commerce and the Arts'.[23] We cannot know how her six-month residence in New Zealand shaped her views of Māori and whether that experience informed the way she judged Aboriginal people. There is evidence to suggest that some colonial women were willing to challenge aspects of the prevailing negative wisdom about Aboriginal cultural practices because of their close proximity to Aboriginal women and children.[24] But we do not know whether Badger came into contact with Aboriginal people often enough or at close enough quarters to likewise question conventional European wisdom. We do know, however, that at Parramatta she found herself living at what Grace Karskens has called 'the centre of cross-cultural meetings and negotiations'.[25] For all its planned European order, Parramatta could not escape its place on the edge of what its inhabitants would have thought of as civilisation. In fact, its position as a frontier town was engrained in its very name, which was a version of 'Burramattagal', the name of the Aboriginal owners of the land on which it was built. Macquarie's intention had been to use the Native Institution as a way of integrating Aboriginal children into European ways of life, to 'civilise' them, by teaching them skills they could use to join the labour force, as well as inducting them into the habits of good, productive Christians. But the steps he took to convince parents to send their children to the institution at the end of 1814 involved hosting a kind of modern corroboree attended by people from many tribes. The first meeting was attended by around sixty people who were fed 'a fine dinner of roast beef, and a cheering jug of ale'.[26] This gathering failed in its objective of recruiting numbers of children, but it was followed by similar events for the next several decades.

This cross-cultural interaction was replicated in other places on the frontier, too. On farms surrounding Parramatta and on the

Hawkesbury, Aboriginal people provided labour to European farmers in exchange for goods or money. As Paul Irish points out, these sorts of reciprocal arrangements 'were neither random nor universal. Aboriginal people formed relationships selectively and strategically, and not all Europeans were inclined to reciprocate.'[27] Aboriginal people were a fact of life for settlers, just as they were for the townsfolk of Sydney, who were used to Aboriginal 'carriers of news and fish; the gossips of the town; the loungers on the quay'.[28] But the relationships that formed were a matter of negotiation, taking place within a context of conflict as well as co-operation, and where acquaintances could become enemies.

But Parramatta was also a military outpost, a defensive bastion built to protect the public farm established at the head of the river. Thomas Humphries and the Veterans were far from the first men garrisoned at Parramatta; they were a continuation of a history of military reinforcement on the frontier that had begun when Arthur Phillip built a redoubt and posted a detachment of soldiers to guard the farm workers and 'prevent any disputes with the natives'.[29] This was perhaps the most telling difference between Badger's experience on the two frontiers: in New Zealand she had been dependent on her hosts, and the small group of Europeans among whom she numbered had no coercive power; now she was embedded with an army whose job was to push back that frontier and impose a new definition of civilisation on the land.

By the time she and Thomas arrived at Parramatta that push-back had been going on for years, to one extent or another. At first, things were quiet, partly as a result of a catastrophic smallpox outbreak that decimated the Aboriginal population on the coast and out onto the plain. But as Aboriginal people began to regroup and as farms began to spread out into the land occupied by the Dharug people to places like Prospect Hill and Toongabbie, violence became a regular occurrence. Over the next decade and a half, violence broke out sporadically, with settlers being attacked on the road, food and clothing being stolen and fields of corn put to the flame around Parramatta and then at Windsor and Richmond Hill. In 1797, in what became known as the Battle of Parramatta, an armed party of settlers tracked Aboriginal leader Pemulwuy and his men in a circle back to the outskirts of the settlement following the plundering of local farms, but 'being fatigued with their march, they entered the town'. What came next, as Pemulwuy attacked his pursuers and the settlers were joined by soldiers from the garrison, was a 'stand-up fight, with flights of spears and at least one volley of musketry, in which five warriors were killed and probably many others wounded'. Pemulwuy himself, described as being 'in a great rage', threw a spear at one of the soldiers before being wounded by musket fire.[30] He survived to trouble settlers for another five years, before being killed in 1802.

The violent struggle that characterised Pemulwuy's war had the same root causes as the co-operation that was to be found on frontier farms. As Europeans fenced off land and brought it under the plough, Aboriginal people's food sources dried up. They could either resist that encroachment or find ways of securing sustenance from the new occupiers; sometimes they did both. During 1805 some Aboriginal people 'solicited to return to Sydney and Parramatta', while others took part in raids.[31] The complex twofold nature of Aboriginal people's reaction to European settlement reflected the situation on the ground where different tribal groups adopted differing strategies, where neighbours could become enemies, and where there existed a 'fine-grained differentiation of friend and foe'.[32] It also meant that Parramatta was not only a place of negotiation but a frontier town surrounded by violence.

By 1814 when Thomas Humphries and Charlotte Badger were Parramatta residents, conflict had moved south-west of Sydney to the Nepean River. But distance from the site of the conflict did not mean the Veterans Company was untouched. That year an 'old soldier' of the company, Isaac Eustace, was killed 'in the district of Appin'. According to the *Sydney Gazette*, he and two other soldiers fired on 'a large body of natives who were plundering the corn fields of a settler, and refused to desist, at the same time making use of every term of provocation and defiance, and in token of a determined spirit, menacing with spears'. A young boy was killed along with Eustace, while the two other soldiers escaped with their lives. Eustace's body was 'found, stripped, and one of the hands taken from the wrist' by a party of fourteen who went in search of the perpetrators. They came upon 'a groupe of the natives, and fired upon them: – they fled, leaving a woman and two children behind them, dead'. The next day, the Aboriginal party made an attack on a stock-keeper, William Baker; he and a woman named Mary Sullivan, generally called Hirburt, were both killed.[33]

As they watched what was happening from Parramatta, Charlotte Badger and her soldier husband must have wondered how long it would be before the violence revisited their neighbourhood and Thomas was drawn into the fray. Their concerns would have been bolstered by the new stage in frontier conflict that erupted in 1815 after years of relative peace, following a drought and consequent food shortages. This time, instead of the small parties that had charac-terised earlier skirmishes, groups of up to four hundred 'mountain natives' (Gandangarra people) launched themselves at out-settlers. The following two years saw a bloody culmination of fighting as violence broke out across the Cumberland Plain. In response, Macquarie launched a full-scale military operation.

At the beginning of April Macquarie set about creating a military cordon across the whole Cumberland Plain, and once again Parramatta became a focus of action. He sent out three parties, each accompanied by Aboriginal guides. The first was to go to Parramatta and then Windsor and then along the Hawkesbury. The second, smaller detachment was to head south-west in the direction of the Cowpastures and wait to link up with the first. The third, commanded by Captain Wallis, headed first for Liverpool and then for Appin, the earlier site of Private Eustace's death, where there had been reports of 'all sorts of outrages and depredations'.[34] Grown men who happened to be killed were to be hanged from trees 'to strike the Survivors with the greater terror'. Women and children were to be spared where possible and taken prisoner instead, and prisoners of both sexes were to be sent to Parramatta and Windsor. Children were to be sent to the Native Institution, now a site of captivity.[35]

While the first two parties stumbled around finding little evidence of the 'hostile natives' they had been sent to quell, the third group found otherwise. After being abandoned by their Aboriginal guides and fruitlessly chasing one Aboriginal sighting after another, Wallis learned of an encampment near Appin. At dawn on 17 April he and his men arrived to find the campsite empty but fires still burning. Then came the cry of a child, which the soldiers followed into the bush. They pushed towards a precipice, 60 metres high; at the barking of dogs, they opened fire. By the end, an estimated fourteen Aboriginal people, including an old man, women and children, lay dead at the bottom of the cliff, or at the soldiers' feet. Only two women and three children survived.

What became known as the Appin massacre sparked the final stage of the frontier wars, even in places that had remained relatively peaceful. At the end of April, only days after the slaughter at Appin, Macquarie sent another detachment of soldiers out to defend a government depot on the new road to the Blue Mountains, via Parramatta, after it became the target of an assault. Again, the officer in charge was instructed to fire on hostile actors and send any prisoners back to Parramatta. By June, trouble had again broken out on the Hawkesbury: two men had been killed and farms were being abandoned.

By that time the governor had changed tack and introduced measures designed to banish Aboriginal people from European settlements. A proclamation in early May announced that armed Aboriginal people were not allowed within a mile of any town or farm, and no more than six Aboriginal people could 'lurk or loiter about any Farm in the Interior'. On the other hand, any Aboriginal people who were willing to become 'regular Settlers' and take up offers of land would be given six months of government stores and the necessary tools and seeds. Those men who did not wish to become farmers were encouraged to take up work as farm labourers 'for those Persons who may be disposed to employ them'. Finally, Macquarie returned to the familiar ground of 'civilising' Aboriginal people by exhorting parents to give their children over to the Native Institution, and 'to embrace so desirable and good an Opportunity of providing for their helpless Offspring and of having them brought up, clothed, fed and educated in a Seminary established for such humane and desirable Purpose'. In furtherance of this goal, he announced an intention to hold 'a general Friendly Meeting of all the Natives residing in the Colony, to take place at the Town of Parramatta, on Saturday the Twenty-eighth of December', where 'the Governor will feel happy to Reward such of them as have given Proofs of Industry, and an inclination to be civilized'.[36]

Fighting continued throughout the rest of the year, but Macquarie's strategy of sending well-equipped detachments across the plain worked, and by November he was able to announce that 'all hostile Operations, Military or other, against the said Native Tribes will cease'.[37] Almost two months later, Parramatta became the site of the final act in the war when the meeting in the town's marketplace went ahead with 179 Aboriginal people, including leaders, in attendance. They sat mostly in a circle on the ground, in the middle of which were placed 'large tables groaning under the weight of roast beef, potatoes, bread, etc, and a large cask of grog'. When Macquarie arrived, he went around the circle 'making himself acquainted with the several tribes, their respective leaders, and residences'. He then assembled the 'chiefs' together 'and confirmed them in the ranks of chieftains to which their own tribes had exalted them, and conferred on them badges of distinction, whereon were engraved their names as chiefs, and those of their tribes'. Next, the fifteen children residing in the Native Institution were paraded in front of the crowd, before the feast began.[38]

By the end Parramatta came to encapsulate every aspect of the war, from confrontation to resolution. It had been the site of direct conflict, of military deployment, of the imprisonment of captives, and of resolution. It had been a frontier town surrounded by violence and the home to the Native Institution, the focus of Macquarie's attempts at 'civilisation'. And while the Veterans Company had not taken an active part in the military response, its members and their wives had been witnesses to all these events, and they had lived with both the threat of confrontation and its aftermath. For residents like Charlotte Badger and Thomas Humphries, Aboriginal people were a fact of daily life, both as a hidden danger and as a presence on the streets. And as inhabitants of a garrison town, they were part of a push outward onto Aboriginal land that enabled the colony to spread across the plain. It was one of the paradoxes of Badger's life that the British authorities who had seen her worthy of expulsion from the wider community now used her services as a wife to support the outward expansion of imperial control. While middle-class officers' wives aided their husbands by hosting guests, showcasing their husband's rank and embodying the ideals of demure femininity that were increasingly at the heart of British culture in all corners of the world, Badger and her sisters provided the logistical domestic support that allowed the army to function, even as they remained subject to its regulation. She was, in a real sense, part of the imperial support crew.[39]

When the war ended, that outward movement swept Badger along with it. At the end of 1820 Humphries was posted to Emu Plains, on the Nepean River near the bottom of the Blue Mountains. The settlement had started out as a depot on the road that Macquarie built across the Cumberland Plain to Bathurst as a way of enforcing his military campaign and securing the land to the west. Now he moved to secure the land by planting a government farm there,

and the Veterans were sent to protect the outpost. The benefits of
the new settlement were twofold: expand and secure the outward
spread of the colony and put convicts to work bolstering the food
supply. In his report on the state of the colony in 1822, John Bigge
described the land at Emu Plains as having 'by far the best soil in
the Colony for Cultivation'.[40] He also described a small settlement
on 800 acres of land cleared for agriculture that consisted of a
brick building for the accommodation of the superintendent of
agriculture and for the governor, when he visited; a store and
granary; accommodation for the storekeeper and the principal
overseer; a convict lock-up; two large crop barns; strong log and
weatherboarded huts for the residence and accommodation of 500
male convicts with kitchen gardens, enclosed and attached to the
huts for the use of the convicts; and barracks for the military. It was
a remote, male-dominated settlement, the latest in a line of isolated
destinations that Badger had made her home in the previous two
decades. That feeling of isolation must have been compounded by the
smallness of the military contingent to which her husband belonged;
according to Bigge, the military guard included only seven privates
of one of the veterans companies and a corporal. And these men
must have been aware that they were in no fit state to deal with any
possible revival in hostilities. Bigge stated that their only purpose
was 'to afford protection to the commisariat store, for the men are
so enfeebled by age as to be incapable of affording resistance even
to an unarmed force'.[41] In December 1820, the same month that
Humphries's detachment arrived, they had a harsh reminder of
their vulnerability. That month fifteen convicts surprised the old
soldiers on the first station on the road to Bathurst, took their
weapons and headed for the Blue Mountains in the belief that
they would find a Dutch settlement and by that means effect their
escape to India.[42] The soldiers must have known that if they could
not withstand convicts then they stood no chance against armed
Aboriginal warriors.

But no such attack ever came. A year later, Charlotte and Thomas were at the far more established settlement of Windsor, and Thomas's time with the Veterans was coming to an end. The colony's military leaders had been lobbying for the end to the company for at least six years before the decision was made to finally send the men to their reward, mostly because of their age and their perceived unfitness for duty. In 1817 Macquarie wrote that:

> . . . the Royal Veteran Company of New South Wales, formed here in 1810 at my own Suggestion on the 102d being relieved by the 73rd Regim't, should be disbanded altogether . . . with the Option of becoming Settlers in Case they should wish to do so; my Reasons for recommending this Measure are that this Veteran Company is now become Almost Altogether In-Effective, the Men being generally quite worn out through long Service, age, or infirmities, and consequently totally unfit to perform even the Common Garrison Duties. The Commissioned and Non-Commissioned Officers and Soldiers are all (with very few Exceptions) Married with large families of Children, all of whom . . . are victualled at the Expence to Government without its deriving any Adequate Advantage therefrom, as twenty five real Effective Soldiers, added to any Regiment which might be Stationed here, would render more Military Service to the Colony than the whole of the Royal Veteran Company, which at present Consists of One Hundred Rank and File; the Expence of Victualling the Women and Children of which is alone Equal at least to that of Victualling the Whole of the Women and Children of a Complete Regiment of the Line.[43]

In 1822 Macquarie's replacement as governor, Thomas Brisbane, made the same plea to his superiors for the same reason:

There is nominally an Invalid Company here, but I beg to
assure you for the Information of His Royal Highness that
there is not one man of them that I consider fit for any Service,
and repeated representations have been made by M. General
Macquarie to have them disbanded, which I should beg to
urge in the strongest terms . . .[44]

It took another year before their request was satisfied and the men
were released from service. The *Sydney Gazette* captured what happened
the day of Thomas Humphries's and his comrades' demobilisation:

The Royal Veteran Company was disembodied on the
24th ult. They were marched from the Barrack-square on
Wednesday se'nnight to the Government-house, under the
command of that worthy old Officer, Captain BRABYN,
where they paraded in the presence of His EXCELLENCY
the COMMANDER of the FORCES, who addressed them
in the kindest manner, with which condescension they were
much gratified. . . . We have no doubt these worthies will be
respected while they live, if only for antiquity's sake. There
are only four that intend to visit Europe, to see whether any
improvements have taken place in their absence worthy of
notice. All the rest have a wish to be interred where their
best days have been spent.[45]

Thomas Humphries was among the majority who wished to
stay and settle in the colony, and six weeks after the company
disbanded, in November 1823, he was given a certificate that
entitled him to a grant of land. Throughout the life of the young
colony planting ex-soldiers in the out-settlements had been 'part of
a broader military strategy' of informally bolstering settlers' defences
around places like Parramatta and beyond, just as stationing them at
outposts had been central to the formal defensive policy.[46] Although

the Veterans were of limited use in open warfare, their knowledge of firearms meant they could be mustered for the defence of their fellow settlers if required. Settling men like Humphries on the land was also intended to turn them into productive, stable citizens who would contribute to the welfare of the colony, so that the act of settling itself became a way of bedding in the society both in physical and cultural terms. In this way they were the same as the ex-convicts who, from the earliest days of the colony, had been given land grants so that 'villains would be turned into villagers'.[47] A new society, not that different from the rural world of England, could be built once former prisoners put down roots in the soil from which families and communities could grow.

Unlike other soldiers, though, Humphries did not receive the grant. Instead, he, his wife and daughter spent the next several years living at either Parramatta or Windsor, moving between the two settlements at which they had lived with the army, while he possibly worked as a blacksmith, the occupation that had been noted on his record of discharge. Evidence suggests that they spent most of the rest of their lives in Windsor, as townsfolk. Here, closer to Sydney and away from the frontier, they left behind the strain of possible attack and the regimen of army life. For perhaps the first time since her arrest in 1796, Charlotte Badger, by now long classified as 'free by servitude', was liberated from the strictures of authority. And at Windsor she found a place where she could make the most of that freedom. In contrast to Parramatta, this settlement had not always been a military town; in fact, it had not started out as a planned settlement at all. Instead, it was the product of mostly men and some women just like Badger: ex-convicts looking to make a new life away from town, away from scrutiny, where the land was good and the crops grew well. Instead of looking out to sea, these settlers found their lives ruled by the rhythm of the river, and they built a new, sometimes riotous culture on its banks. Windsor was known as 'a little sporting town', where cockfighting, bare-knuckled brawling and horse racing were popular pastimes. The local Killarney Races were remembered as 'rollicking festivals of boozing, betting, fun and enjoyment – the booths at Killarney were crowded with people, black and white, drinkers, dancers and tambourine players. . . . In the evening a great bonfire licked the starry night sky beside the river, Windsor was alive with music and a ball was held in the town square, while drunken soldiers picked fights with the Aboriginal men of the "Mulgoa tribe".'[48] Macquarie had made it his mission to bring order to this place, officially proclaiming it a town in 1810 and setting the architects and builders to work on a church, courthouse and inn that still help to give the town its historical feel today, although it retained its reputation as a centre of popular entertainment and rowdy behaviour despite his efforts. Macquarie also ordered the building of barracks to house the soldiers stationed at Windsor to fight the wars waged by him and his predecessors, wars that had brought the likes of Thomas Humphries. By the 1820s those wars were over and the settlement originally called Green Hills was being joined by new towns along the Hawkesbury and further afield, such as Lower Portland Head, and a road was being built by convicts into the nearby Macdonald Valley.

It was while he was residing at Windsor in 1829 that Humphries made one last attempt to become a settler. In December that year he wrote to Governor Darling saying that he had previously been given an order allowing him to select 100 acres of land. He had sent his request to the Assistant Surveyor but nothing more had happened, and he now asked that if the order had been lost that a new one be issued so that he could take up the offer.[49] The reply came that before his request could be granted he would have to undertake to cultivate the land and take up residence on it, and enter into a bond to that effect.[50]

From here on, the trail goes cold for a decade. Perhaps the idea of having to cultivate 100 acres of land was too much for a seventy-year-old to face, or perhaps he got his land but the record has been lost. The likely explanation, though, is that he remained landless, given that in 1843 he and Badger were still in Windsor.

That year, when she was sixty-five years old, the freedom from official scrutiny that Badger appears to have enjoyed for twenty years came to an inexplicable end. On 13 May she was charged with larceny and was bailed to appear on 5 July. At the trial Michael Cotton and Jane Oliver acted as witnesses for the Crown, Cotton being a local constable and Oliver presumably the victim of the crime. Thomas Humphries, along with Robert Sinkings and David Brown, provided sureties and apparently acted as witnesses for the defence. Sinkings was a former convict and cabinetmaker, while Brown was a carpenter. In the court documents, Humphries was by this time described as a householder. Unlike at her first court appearance in 1796, this time Badger was found not guilty and was discharged.[51]

During her time at Windsor, then, Badger had gone from being on the cusp of landholding respectability to lapsing into a past she had seemingly escaped, even if she ultimately avoided the judgment of the court. We do not know why this lapse occurred, or what prompted the charges to be brought. Perhaps, as had possibly been the case with Benjamin Wright, there had been a breakdown in a pre-existing personal or professional relationship between her and Oliver. Perhaps she was attempting to reclaim goods she considered to be her own. We also do not know what she was accused of stealing, only that she was charged. But after a lifetime in New South Wales of seeming to avoid the eye of the law, her old age was marred by an incident that must have been a harrowing reminder of the events that had brought her to the other side of the world in the first place, for a reason we will never know or understand. What this episode also suggests is that she ultimately failed to overcome the judgment of her social betters by building a life of quiet, untroublesome progress. While most former convicts could not realistically hope to become Simeon Lord or even Solomon

Wiseman, the Hawkesbury hotelier and entrepreneur whose life was the inspiration for Kate Grenville's book *The Secret River*, they could look at more modest social advancement and capital accumulation through land ownership, even if they could never quite escape the convict 'stain'. Instead, by remaining a member of Windsor's townsfolk, and relapsing into the ignominy of a court appearance, Badger confirmed the suspicions about convict women held by her social superiors.

Whatever the cause of this brush with the authorities, this is the last point at which we can know for sure what was happening in the lives of Charlotte Badger and her husband. The 1841 census listed a Thomas Humphries living at George Street, Windsor, and a man of that name died in Windsor in December 1843 at the age of ninety-two, at least ten years older than Charlotte's husband would have been at the time. It is probable that this man was, in fact, another Thomas Humphries, a shoemaker and former convict born in 1760 who arrived on the *Guildford* in 1811. If so, then we know nothing of the fate of either Badger or her husband, given that no similar death records can be found for them. There are no recorded deaths for a woman of that name in New South Wales, and no clues are to be found in looking for her daughter, either. We do not know if Maria married and had children, and whether Charlotte ever became a grandmother, or where she spent the remainder of her old age, or how much of it she spent alone.

In the absence of any conclusive answers, we leave her living north-west of Sydney in the aftermath of war on a frontier made and ultimately conquered by men from the army into which she had married, looking back at a life that had taken her across the world, from a rural town in England to another one on the Hawkesbury River, still a member of society's lower class, still the object of suspicion from those above her in social ranking but having experienced things of which her Worcestershire family could only dream. The Bromsgrove girl had become a convict, a runaway, a cultural emissary and a wife and mother. All because of four guineas and a Queen Anne's half-crown.

The
Histories
of
Charlotte Badger

Even today, in the age of long-haul plane travel, the trip from London to Sydney and on to Auckland is gruelling. Anyone who has completed that trip in economy class can attest to the physical discomfort that comes with being confined to a cramped space for more than a day and the mental fortitude it takes to stave off the idea that the journey will simply never end.

I made my own version of that trip in search of Charlotte Badger. In 2016 I went from Auckland to London and then to Worcester to find records of her early life and imprisonment. Having previously studied only New Zealand subjects, I was pleasantly surprised by how often a woman of such low birth appeared in the record and thanked the assiduous officials of the English civil service for keeping such a close eye on the population. In London I found the Home Office records of her crime and commutation of her death sentence; in Worcester I found references to her dirty clothing and good behaviour in the logs written by local magistrates after their regular visits to the gaol. A few months after arriving home, I went to Sydney to hunt for her in the New South Wales state library and state archive, and found evidence of her marriage to Thomas Humphries and his postings on the frontier.

So, in my own way, and in reverse, I recreated the trips she took from England to the other side of the world and from New South Wales to New Zealand and back, following her from one side of the globe to the other. But even as I did so I was constantly reminded of the distances between us. Firstly, of course, was the speed of our travel, which was itself a manifestation of the obvious temporal space that divided us. The nineteen-hour flight from Auckland to Dubai before immediately carrying on to London was an act of endurance by contemporary standards, but it was nothing compared to the months of sea-voyaging she survived. And while my trips left behind a fulsome digital footprint as I crossed borders, checked into hotels, went shopping, kept in touch with family and friends, took photographs and wrote a travel blog, Badger's travels, for all the good work of those civil servants, still failed to leave behind many clues about her day-to-day life. Her movements were recorded mostly when she transgressed; thanks to the pervasive nature of English CCTV, mine were recorded as soon as I left my hotel room. The result is that, despite tracing her footsteps, visiting the town of her birth and unearthing evidence of her fate, she remains, in many ways, a mystery to me, and the doubt surrounding her persists.

Still, we can reconstruct the basic shape of her life, and in doing so we can dispel some of the myths that have grown up around her. We can be sure that she was born in Bromsgrove, was sentenced to seven years' transportation for breaking into Benjamin Wright's house in 1796 and spent four years in Worcester County Gaol before being sent to New South Wales at the end of 1800. We can also be sure that she was on board the *Venus* when it sailed first to Van Diemen's Land and then the Bay of Islands in 1806, and that she returned to Sydney via Norfolk Island in mid-1807. We also know that she married Thomas Humphries in 1811 and was still with him at Windsor in 1843.

Establishing these basic facts allows us to eliminate the fanciful possibility that she was a pirate who escaped New Zealand and made her way to North America via Tonga, disappointing though this might be. But other more mundane elements of doubt remain. We do not know anything for sure about the nature of her relationship with Wright or why she chose to steal from him, or how she spent her first five years in New South Wales and whether that involved spending time in the Female Factory, or why she was on board the *Venus* to begin with, or what happened to her shipmates. Neither can we know what happened to her first child, or to Maria, or even establish with certainty just how many children she had, and we can't be sure when and how she died or where she is buried. If we cannot establish such basic things as births and deaths then how can we say we really know anything about a person's life at all, and what is the value of telling that person's story if such fundamental things as these are missing?

Adding to these simple gaps is the lack of our emotional understanding. We cannot know the shock of being sentenced to death, or the mixed feelings that came with commutation followed by years of imprisonment and then transportation. Nor can we comprehend Badger's response to finding herself living on the coast of a strange land in a culture so different from anything she had experienced before. We do not know how she made sense of her life, how she reconciled the loss of her original home, followed by the loss of her child, and whether the life she built in New South Wales compensated for or improved on the one she left behind. In all these fundamental ways she remains beyond our reach, a person lost to time and silence.

What's more, if some of the reasons that we have been drawn to her life are thrown into doubt, or are unlikely to be accurate, then isn't her place in the historical narrative undermined? It is easy to stake a claim in history if you were, in fact, Australia's only woman pirate; it is much harder to do so if you were a convict and an army wife who experienced one twelve-month period of extreme adventure before slipping back into obscurity.

But all is not lost. We do have ways of making sense of her and of securing her place in history. The story of Badger's life told here presents her as a woman whose travels coincided with various stages of life, each of which tells us something about the time in which she lived, from the treatment of petty criminals in late-eighteenth-century England, to the early penal colony of New South Wales, to the early contact period in New Zealand, and the outward spread of Sydney following frontier conflict. This study has claimed her as someone whose life can illuminate the past and is worthy of biographical treatment, despite the doubt that continues to envelop her.

Traditionally, historians have viewed biography as the poor relation to 'real' history writing.[1] Those criticisms mostly centre on the narrowness of a biography's focus and the ability or otherwise of an individual life to illustrate anything helpful about the past. Criticisms have also highlighted biographers' reluctance to engage with social and cultural historiography that might overshadow the telling of their subject's tale. One rebuttal to this is to say that history is, after all, just a collection of lives: 'Individual lives do not encompass all history, but despite their messiness, obscurity and fictions, individual lives are the stitches of the past. There would be no fabric of history without them and sometimes we can only really feel the past one thread at a time.'[2]

Another response has been the move to tell the life stories of people who have not traditionally warranted a life history but whose lives tell us something significant about the culture that produced them so that they become 'a world in a life and a life in the world'.[3] While acknowledging biography's traditional place at the margin of historical study, it has been asserted that 'biography is . . . seen to offer ways of throwing new light on a range of different historical periods and problems and of bringing individuals and groups who had previously been ignored into the framework of historical analysis'.[4] Biography has been used by feminist and some postcolonial historians as a way of putting 'ordinary people' at the centre of history: 'these forms of history share a concern to explore the activities, experience and historical agency of groups with relatively little political and economic power or social status and to locate and listen to the voices of those who had been silenced in earlier historical writing'.[5] In this analysis the lives and actions of 'ordinary' people become vital.

While aspects of Badger's life certainly raise her above the level of the 'ordinary' and propel her into a national narrative, her status as an illiterate woman of low birth and the resultant poverty of source material about her mean that her story cannot be told in a traditional way, and that we have to revise our definition of what constitutes a biography. We have to abandon our desire to understand her thoughts and feelings and focus instead on the wider meaning of her life, and in doing so we have to acknowledge the impossibility of understanding how each phase of her life affected her sense of 'personhood'. When we do, we enlarge the ways in which we can understand the past as well as the practice of historical writing, so that she is worthy not just of a place in New Zealand's national biography but worthy of a history in her own right.

It was a life that allows us to understand the many situations and locations in which she found herself and the mobility that caused her to move from one place to another. It is important to recognise, though, that viewing her in this way, as a mobile person and as someone worthy of a biographical history, is itself a result of historical developments and the changing ways in which we as inhabitants of the present have decided to look upon and think about the past. This has always been the case with Badger's story; each generation of writers, of both fiction and non-fiction, who have discovered her have reinterpreted her to fit the times, and each version of the story has contributed to the next, including this one. All of these changes have shaped the histories of Charlotte Badger that have been told. If we think of the stories of Badger's life, from her conviction for housebreaking to her more fanciful leadership role in the *Venus* mutiny and her fictional escape to Tonga, as the result of a series of tellings and retellings, then those retellings themselves have a history that explains how and why they came about in the way they did.

These changes in the way her story has been told are particularly evident when we look at three themes that run through it: the treatment of female convicts, the New Zealand frontier, and her place in the New Zealand national narrative.

When Louis Becke told his story about the *Venus*, Badger and Hagerty were members of a riotous, drunken group of convicts and crew, with the women themselves portrayed almost as harlots, entertaining Kelly with a 'dancing exhibition'. To an extent this portrayal is just a reflection of Becke's storytelling, which was full of rapscallions and outsiders. His stories of Australia and the Pacific were peopled by 'devils' and 'beasts' as a way of entertaining his increasingly urbanised audience for whom such characters were objects of fascination from a world they would never see. But his portrayal of Badger and Hagerty owed something to earlier stories of female Caribbean pirates, in particular Anne Bonny and Mary Read, who 'cursed and swore like sailors, carried their weapons like those well trained in the ways of war, and boarded prize vessels as only the most daring and respected members of pirate crews were permitted to do'. Read and Bonny had dressed as men as they stole a sloop at Nassau, and then continued to harass ships in the waters off Jamaica, before being captured in 1720 and taken for trial.[6] Their adventures featured in *A General History of the Pyrates*, published in 1724, 'at a time when the sphere of social action for women was narrowing'.[7] By the time Becke came to tell his own tale of female pirates, women's expected behaviour had long been defined by the ideas of respectability and virtue exemplified by Samuel Marsden's earlier attitudes towards female convicts. Becke's treatment of Badger and Hagerty was much less censorious than Marsden's would have been, but it was still coloured by the nineteenth century's idea of the 'damned whore' whose behaviour set her apart from the feminine ideal. And his willingness to equate Badger and Hagerty's mutinous behaviour with sexual brazenness reflected a tendency to view female disorder in sexualised terms, particularly in spaces dominated by men, including on board ships.[8]

When the story was retold in the *Sydney Morning Herald* during the 1930s, those elements of judgment remained. Badger was described as being 'less sympathetic' than other convict women who had risen above their low status and made good commercially. Her behaviour marked her out as morally problematic even before she got on board the *Venus*. Describing her as a 'London pickpocket' meant that this retelling aligned her with the women from the capital whom Governor King had marked out for particular opprobrium over a hundred years earlier. Then, once the ship was under way, 'the buxom Charlotte' was the cause of poor Kelly's ruination after she seduced him. But something new was going on here, too. By the 1920s a new cultural figure had appeared on the scene: the 'modern girl'. She followed the 'new woman' of the late nineteenth and early twentieth centuries who was associated with women's social and political activism, including the suffrage movement. While the idea of the new woman could be used as a caricature by which to mock women activists, the modern girl 'was sassy and strong-willed, less docile and domesticated than the old woman, but less political than the new woman. She achieved a different relationship with her suitors through high-spiritedness and force of personality, not by attending meetings and lobbying for legislative reform.'[9] The *Herald* story described Badger as 'a rather good-looking young woman who possessed a violent temper', while the illustration that accompanied it showed a slim young woman dressed in men's clothing behind the ship's wheel. This portrayal, as well as drawing on the idea of the modern girl, also had real-life corollaries in

the forms of adventuring women such as Jean Batten and Amelia
Earhart who embodied the modernity of the post-First World War
era.[10] By the 1930s, then, a glamorous Badger had emerged, with
her willingness to set her own course and seize her independence
while, quite literally, wearing the trousers.

But the stereotype of the slatternly female convict persisted, as
did the idea of convicts more generally being members of a criminal
class. Attempts were made from the 1920s to overturn this view and
replace the criminal with 'admirable political rebels and morally
innocent village Hampdens' who 'suffered the effects of a relentless
and uncaring policy instigated by the British aristocracy to protect
their property, wealth and privileges'. But even here, 'The nobility of
suffering, the injustice, the miseries, the fearsome cruelties, did not
include the convicted women.'[11] Female convicts would have to wait
until the 1970s before writers became interested in making them the
subjects of serious investigation. The resulting histories, powered by
the women's liberation movement, were 'Angry in tone, unforgiving
in attitude, and intent on revolutionary change'; they were determined
to write women into history, but initially at least tended to focus on
convict women as objects of oppression and as 'victims of victims'.[12]
Over the next few decades, the field of women's history expanded
to tell the story of a range of contemporary concerns, including
women's economic participation and resistance to authority. Focusing
on women convicts' work, historians like Deborah Oxley reframed
them as skilled contributors to society rather than as oppressed sexual
objects, condemned to enforced whoredom in the convict colonies
and to serve as breeders in the new nation.[13] Joy Damousi re-examined
disorderly behaviour as a way of thinking about how 'ideas about
masculinity, femininity, and sexuality are shaped and defined and how
convict women dealt with their relationships with the convict men and
their commanders in order to be autonomous and create a space for
themselves'.[14] Kay Daniels, meanwhile, set out to 'reveal the diversity
of female convict spaces, relationships and reactions on one hand and

the complex nuances of the ever-evolving structures of control on the other'.[15] The result was that convicts became part of the 'range of women in the past, Indigenous and non-Indigenous, urban and rural, famous and unknown' who were written into Australian history in a variety of ways.[16]

The writing of women's experiences that followed the second wave of feminism in the 1970s had a similar effect in New Zealand as writers in the 1990s noted, 'Over the past fifteen years or so, women have begun to make an appearance in New Zealand history'.[17] Although the rehabilitation of female convicts was obviously missing, attention was given to the expectation of respectability that was visited upon women of all classes, as well as to those who failed to meet this expectation.[18] Charlotte Macdonald, for example, wrote critically for the first time about young single female immigrants whose failure to meet society's behavioural standards marked them out as being 'bad characters'. These women, like female convicts, had been treated as vectors of vice, specifically prostitution: 'the idea that a significant number of young women migrants took up prostitution when they arrived was never entirely dispelled'.[19] When the Dictionary of New Zealand Biography was published in 1990, Charlotte Badger fitted into this category of supposedly troublesome women. In explaining why Badger deserved her place, Mary Louise Ormsby wrote:

> Charlotte Badger's story is dramatic and unique; in some respects, however, she foreshadows a later group of women immigrants, whom poverty prevented from conforming to the contemporary stereotype of feminine respectability. Among them were those who, like Charlotte Badger, reacted to their situation with defiance and courage.[20]

When Barbara Brookes came to write her into the history of New Zealand women twenty-five years later, Badger was still the victim of eighteenth-century poverty. It was that lack of means that had forced her into housebreaking, followed by the exile that eventually brought her to the New Zealand coast.[21]

Over time, then, Badger has gone from being an example of female transgression to someone who has benefited from the reassessment of female convicts and working-class women generally that has taken place over the past fifty years. In the process someone once described as less worthy of sympathy than other women has become a figure of 'defiance and courage'. The portrayal of Badger here borrows from and builds on those developments. We can now see her as being in many ways typical of female transportees as a young single woman sentenced to seven years, as a woman in some kind of common law relationship and as a mother. And while she, like her fellow early female convicts, was subject to both the harsh system of justice that sent her to New South Wales in the first place and the moral judgment of colonial officials and elite society, she was neither an embodiment of transgression nor someone without ways of making her way in life, as much of the rest of her time with Humphries suggests.

A similar evolution emerges when we look at another theme running through the written histories of Badger's life; namely, the frontier. Becke's treatment of the New Zealand frontier is similar to his portrayal of Badger and Hagerty as pirates in that as a teller of tall tales he had a propensity for playing up danger and adventure. It was a propensity which saw him depict New Zealand as a place of refuge but also of peril. In Becke's telling, Benjamin Kelly managed to persuade Māori to give him and his companions shelter, but in return he took part in 'a warlike excursion with his Maori friends', and his story of Badger's trip to Tonga involved her escaping from 'captivity with the Maoris'.[22] In some ways Becke's liking for this brand of storytelling reflected his own experience as a blackbirder, smuggler and gun-runner for Bully Hayes, which had led to him standing trial for piracy. But he was also part of a generation of writers who favoured the 'yarn' tradition of storytelling that recaptured 'the old times' before the frontier had been rolled back and replaced by towns and cities. In Australia fiction writers such as Rolf Boldrewood were telling tales of bushrangers, while in New Zealand 'old identities' like John Webster were recounting their lives of adventure during the early colonial period when they lived alongside Māori. Several decades later they would be followed by James Cowan, one of the most popular historical writers in early twentieth-century New Zealand, who peopled the landscape with Māori and Pākehā. He collected stories from places he experienced first-hand as he travelled the country and bundled those stories into anthologies that conveyed a sense of adventure from 'the old days', seeing himself 'as a gatherer of narratives of a not-quite-vanquished past'.[23] What these stories, including Becke's narrative about the *Venus*, had in common was that they reached back into the past to tell tales for a European audience for whom the frontier, including its indigenous inhabitants, was tantalisingly close and yet far enough away so as not to threaten their settled lives.

By the 1960s, for some popular chroniclers the New Zealand frontier had gone from a place of dangerous adventure to outright bloodshed, from the *Boyd* massacre in 1809 to the attack on the *Harriet* involving Betty Guard in 1834. The treatment of the *Venus* crew in *The Brown Frontier* and *Coasts of Treachery*, which borrowed narrative elements from Becke's story, fits into this category. In *The Brown Frontier* in particular, Badger and her companions were harbingers of destruction, as indicated by the book's repetition of Samuel Marsden's report that the ship carried on down the coast after leaving the Bay of Islands, kidnapping local women as it went: 'In the blood-stained annals of the early contacts between white man and brown throughout the Pacific, there is surely no more striking example of the dictum that the evil that men do lives after them than that provided by the men of the *Venus* on the coast of New Zealand. From the day the brig first touched at North Cape, the pattern of death and disaster for which her lawless crew was responsible began to take shape.'[24] According to the author, C. W. Vennell, Badger and the *Venus* people were among the worst Europe had to offer, but they had been replaced by better stock. Now, with 'fear and hate . . . gone for ever', tales of savagery could be revisited from a position of safety and surety that Māori and Pākehā were peacefully reconciled to each other in a land where, as far as these writers were concerned, the question of who had ultimately won the argument had been answered.[25]

When it came to Badger's inclusion in the Dictionary of New Zealand Biography in 1990 and her subsequent appearance in scholarly histories, assigning her such a simplistic role in New Zealand's past was no longer sustainable. In the interim, the country's history had been pushed in a new direction following the mobilisation of Māori political concerns, often referred to as the 'Māori renaissance', and then by the emergence of the idea of biculturalism following the Treaty of Waitangi settlement process and a growing emphasis on the idea of a Treaty partnership in public life. Meanwhile, historians such as Judith Binney had been describing a pre-colonial and colonial New Zealand where Māori and Pākehā were entwined in each other's lives,[26] and were contributing to a growing international literature that would see cultural change in terms of 'a two-way process of exchange and dialogue'.[27] New Zealand was still a place of contestation, but the focus now was on renegotiating the ways in which that contest was understood. Badger's Dictionary entry might have emphasised her role as the forerunner to single female immigrants, but she also represented the 'cross-cultural entanglement' that became the focus of such works as Anne Salmond's *Between Worlds* and Vincent O'Malley's *The Meeting Place*. These were, of course, far more scholarly than many of the earlier treatments of Badger, but they borrowed from and reused those treatments to present her as an early cultural agent, as someone who represented 'cross-cultural trial and error' at a time when the relationship between Māori and Pākehā was being re-evaluated.[28]

The part of her life that Badger spent in New Zealand that is presented in this study reflects these later developments. We do not know the extent to which she was enmeshed in the community at Wairoa Bay, but we can say that she was a participant in early cultural engagement, on Māori terms. The frontier described here was not one of wanton violence or savagery or of raucous adventure. It was a place where Māori agency and decision-making dominated but where rangatira might make alliances with Pākehā for their mutual benefit. It is a frontier that has emerged in the past several decades as Māori and Pākehā New Zealanders have re-examined their shared past, and where Māori agency has been given greater consideration by Pākehā historians, including me.[29]

The way in which Badger's life in Parramatta and Emu Plains is covered here reflects similar changes in Australia. From the 1970s and 1980s, in keeping with critical reassessments taking place in other former settler colonies and in the wake of Aboriginal rights protests, the Australian frontier became a place where Aboriginal people, once consigned to obscurity in the face of supposedly triumphant white settlement, were active players, in acts of both resistance and engagement. The history of dispossession and displacement of Aboriginal people took its place alongside that of white settlement, but that story of displacement has been complicated by the acknowl-edgement that the original inhabitants of the land did not fade away and just accept their fate. Badger's time on the Australian frontier can be told from the point of view of sustained conflict because of the relatively recent assertion that what took place on the outskirts of Sydney in the opening decades of white settlement was, in fact, warfare.[30]

These reassessments of the history of contact between indigenous people and settlers in New Zealand and Australia have become part of ongoing debates about national identity in both countries, as they have tried to come to grips with histories of dispossession in the hope of reconciliation.[31] In Badger's case it has been her role as a cultural emissary more than any other that has allowed her to make regular appearances in New Zealand's national story from the 1990s, including Belich's general history, as the narrative has shifted to include examples of early cultural engagement. In recent years, though, there has been a growing interest in looking at the country not only as a nation in its own right but as a former part of the British Empire. This re-emergence of interest in an empire that most thought was dead and gone followed on from the type of reassessment of the colonial past in former colonies that had also taken place in New Zealand and Australia. As well as studying the way power was wielded in those places, historians began to reimagine the empire itself and how its component parts worked together. Where until the 1980s, the empire was viewed in terms of a 'spoked wheel . . . where lines of communications, finance and personnel radiate out from London to each colony in the periphery',[32] from the 1990s it came to be seen as a web or a network that connected not just one colony to the core, but multiple colonies to each other. It was described as 'a "bundle of relationships" that brought disparate regions, communities and individuals into contact through systems of mobility and exchange'.[33] This focus on exchange has gone hand in hand with an interest in the movement of people: 'Mobility has become one of the key themes of new imperial history writing as scholars trace the movement of people, things and ideas across imperial spaces and national boundaries, exploring the networks that lay at the heart of imperial endeavour.'[34]

This view of the empire has informed this study of Badger and accounts for its interest in and emphasis on her mobility. Indeed, we can easily view hers as a life shaped by the empire. She travelled to New South Wales on board a ship that had worked in the service of the East India Company. Once there, she took up residence in a settlement that resulted from the disaster at Yorktown in 1781 but which was now benefiting from the end of the company's monopoly on whaling, which in turn helped shore up the loss of

British whaling bases in Massachusetts. That settlement was also benefiting from the sealing industry, which harvested furs for sale in China in return for tea. It was this trade that was directly responsible for Badger's sojourn in New Zealand on board a sealing ship built in Calcutta. As a Sydney resident she also lived on a continent that had come to Britain's attention during trips of exploration that identified the value of the Pacific breadfruit as a way of feeding Caribbean slaves. And Badger's own husband, of course, had served in an army dedicated to defending those slave colonies before being sent to New South Wales to protect a different type of imperial outpost, while she provided logistical support in the form of domestic duties. In all these ways, Badger's life was touched by the expansion of British power and commerce. Viewing her from this perspective, though, is a direct result not only of the currents of her own life but of the tides of history-writing and the way we have chosen to make sense of our own world.

That world includes not only the aftermath of an empire that led to mass migration but the broader phenomenon of globalisation. At a time where almost every aspect of our lives, from the clothes we wear and the goods we buy to the news we consume and how we spend our leisure time, reflects our interconnectedness with the rest of the world, there has been an emphasis on digging into the history of globalisation itself. Here, again, the movement of people has become a focus of attention, as historians have tracked individual paths across the world, as well as the growth of commerce and economic power.[35] Badger's brief involvement with the international whaling trade and the routes the ships took, including from Sydney and New Zealand across the Pacific and to North America, allows us to see her as someone whose life was touched by global forces that went beyond the imperial, and as someone whose life, in a sense, was a forerunner to our own.

It is this ability to put her life to work in a variety of ways and to keep reinterpreting her in ways that speak to us that keeps her alive as a historical figure. When we look at Charlotte Badger's life, we see ourselves looking back. The choices we make about her, how we reconstruct the glimpses we have of her, the histories we choose to tell, whether we see her as a cultural emissary or a tiny player on a global stage, reveal something about how we see our own world. Just as writers such as Louis Becke took her life and used it to tell fictionalised stories that reflected the time in which they lived, so we continue to interpret her life in ways that help explain our own lived experiences, both local and global.

This helps to explain why she remains the subject of songs and visual culture, and why she speaks to audiences beyond those readers and writers of history interested in questions of national identity or global mobility. Of course, the details of her life, or at least the version that we think we know, as a pirate, a captive and a traveller, make for compelling material, as does the mystery that has surrounded her fate. But beyond that, we are drawn to her because of the determined individuality she seems to represent. Perhaps, like Louis Becke's urbanised readers at the end of the nineteenth century, we respond to someone who, as James Belich put it, 'claw[ed] her way from so many frying pans and fires'.[36] In a world of settled daily routine, she represents what we want the past to be: a place of adventure, just out of reach. She also seems to embody a kind of womanhood we are more comfortable with, especially in the wake of third-wave feminism. The determination to buck authority and exploit her sexuality found in the stories of her pirate adventures fits with that movement's emphasis on individual female autonomy, which 'unsettle[s] essentialist narratives about dominant men and passive women' and presents an idea of femininity that is 'simultaneously authentic, playful, and part of the . . . project of reclamation' of female choice and power.[37] We are more willing to give her latitude for the kind of behaviour for which previous generations would have judged her harshly. Stripped of the judgment found in places like the *Sydney Morning Herald* that she was 'less sympathetic' than her more well-behaved sisters, we allow ourselves to celebrate her in all her feisty, pistol-wielding glory. This is the Badger we see in Xoë Hall's piece on the cover of this book, the latest in a series of original visual representations of her. Here she is a literally colourful, appealing character festooned with the imagery of her equally colourful life. She is a woman of strength and power, which the artist symbolises by the inclusion of a taniwha.

The person at the heart of all these stories, of all these histories, differs in many ways knowable and unknowable from the woman who was sentenced to transportation, sojourned in New Zealand and returned to New South Wales, but our retelling of her history, in all its forms, has allowed her to experience a life beyond the grave that eludes virtually everyone born into her modest circumstances. In turn, she has given us a window both into the past and, in the stories we choose to tell, into ourselves.

Notes

Introduction

1 Ormsby, 'Badger, Charlotte', https://teara.govt.nz/en/biographies/1b1/badger-charlotte
2 This restaurant is Charlotte's Kitchen in Paihia.
3 Gloria, 'Charlotte Badger', www.youtube.com/watch?v=fuGlWBAMBZ0; Jack Hayter, 'Charlotte Badger', www.youtube.com/watch?v=5x5pr_KfuDM. See also 'Ballad of Charlotte Badger', cited in Duffield, '"Haul Away the Anchor Girls"', pp. 35–36.
4 'Charlotte Badger', https://lesterhall.com/kiwiana/charlotte-badger.htm
5 Parry, *Vagabonds*.
6 Reihana, 'Nomads of the Sea', 2019, www.lisareihana.com/nomads-of-the-sea.
7 Badger, *Charlotte Badger: Buccaneer*.
8 Mantel, 'The Iron Maiden', http://downloads.bbc.co.uk/radio4/reith2017/reith_2017_hilary_mantel_lecture2.pdf
9 Mantel, 'The Day is for the Living', http://downloads.bbc.co.uk/radio4/reith2017/reith_2017_hilary_mantel_lecture1.pdf
10 Mantel, 'The Day is for the Living', http://downloads.bbc.co.uk/radio4/reith2017/reith_2017_hilary_mantel_lecture1.pdf
11 Junod, 'The Falling Man'.

The Accused

1 Gwilliam, *Old Worcester*, p. 15.
2 See, for example, *Sydney Morning Herald*, 26 October 1937, p. 21; Vennell, *The Brown Frontier*, p. 19.
3 Laird, *Topographical and Historical Description of the County of Worcester*, www.parishmouse.co.uk/worcestershire/bromsgrove-worcestershire-family-history-guide
4 'Nail Making in Bromsgrove', http://bromsgrovenailmaking.wixsite.com/nail-making/untitled-c139r
5 Griffin, *Liberty's Dawn*, p. 55.
6 Griffin, p. 83.
7 Kirkby, *Child Labour in Britain*, p. 28.
8 *Bromsgrove Rousler*, no. 17, 2002, p. 7.
9 Duffield, '"Haul Away the Anchor Girls"', p. 39.
10 Index of Apprentices Indentures.

11   Wright, Worcestershire Original Wills Part 2 1694–1857.
12   Housebreaking can be defined as '[b]reaking into a dwelling house in the day time with intent to commit a felony (normally theft), or actually doing so, thereby putting the inhabitants of the house in fear'. See Old Bailey Proceedings Online, www.oldbaileyonline.org/static/Crimes.jsp#housebreaking
13   Emsley, *Crime and Society in England*, p. 164.
14   King, *Crime, Justice, and Discretion in England*, ch. 2.
15   See King, *Crime and Law in England*, ch. 5; King, *Crime, Justice, and Discretion in England*, pp. 196–207, 278–88.
16   Grand larceny, which was punishable by death, was defined as the theft of goods to the value of 1 shilling or more. Badger stole an amount significantly higher than this, and with the aggravating circumstances of housebreaking, which was charged as a separate crime. See, for example, www.oldbaileyonline.org/static/Crimes.jsp#grandlarceny
17   Badger, *Charlotte Badger: Buccaneer*, p. 38.
18   County of Worcester Quarter Sessions Order Books.
19   Stern, 'The Bread Crisis in Britain', pp. 171–72; Davis, 'Bread Riots, Britain, 1795'.
20   Emsley, p. 33.
21   Honeyman, *Child Workers in England*, pp. 15–16.
22   King, *Crime, Justice, and Discretion in England*, p. 150.
23   See also Cox, *Crime in England 1688–1815*, p. 44; Emsley, pp. 25, 33.
24   King, *Crime, Justice, and Discretion in England*, pp. 201–3.
25   Oxley, *Convict Maids*, p. 49.
26   Oxley, p. 47.
27   Emsley, p. 99. See also, King, *Crime and Law in England*, p. 171.
28   King, *Crime, Justice, and Discretion in England*, p. 207.
29   King, *Crime, Justice, and Discretion in England*, pp. 201–7, 285.
30   Green, *The History and Antiquities of the City and Suburbs of Worcester*, p. 8.
31   Duman, cited in Cox, p. 27.
32   Cox, p. 108.
33   Cox, p. 107.
34   King and Ward, 'Rethinking the Bloody Code in Eighteenth-Century Britain', pp. 159–205.
35   James Neild, *State of the Prisons in England, Scotland, and Wales*, p. 597.
36   Neild, p. 597.
37   Neild, p. 594.
38   Thomas, 'The real Little Dorrit: Charles Dickens and the debtors' prison', https://media.nationalarchives.gov.uk/index.php/the-real-little-dorrit-charles-dickens-and-the-debtors-prison
39   Neild, p. 595.
40   Petition of the Prisoners for Debt in the County Gaol of Worcester.
41   County Gaol Visiting Magistrates Minutes, 13 January 1807.
42   County Gaol Visiting Magistrates Minutes, [n.d.] April 1796.
43   County Gaol Visiting Magistrates Minutes, 3 May 1796.
44   County Gaol Visiting Magistrates Minutes, 3 May 1796.
45   County Gaol Visiting Magistrates Minutes, 20 August 1796.
46   County Gaol Visiting Magistrates Minutes, 15 February 1797.

47   County Gaol Visiting Magistrates Minutes, 22 February 1797.
48   County Gaol Visiting Magistrates Minutes, 7 July 1797.
49   County Gaol Visiting Magistrates Minutes, 31 January 1799.
50   To the Visiting Justices at Worcester, 16 October 1798, HO 13/12, National Archives, London.
51   Mayfield was also known as Hannah Maywell.
52   County Gaol Visiting Magistrates Minutes, 27 November 1800.
53   Hughes, *The Fatal Shore*, p. 38.
54   Dickens, *Sketches by Boz*, ch. xxv.

The Convict

1   Bateson, *The Convict Ships*, pp. 70–72.
2   *Historical Records of Australia* (HRA), series 1, vol. 2, note 153, p. 733. Bateson states that they were infected with typhoid. See p. 167.
3   Robert Scott, Letters, 1800–1802, 2 September 1800.
4   Robinson, *The Women of Botany Bay*, pp. 21, 29.
5   Cunningham, *Two Years in New South Wales*, p. 272.
6   Damousi, *Depraved and Disorderly*, p. 16.
7   Smith, *A Cargo of Women*, p. 51.
8   Cunningham, p. 275.
9   Anna Josepha King journal of a voyage from England to Australia in the ship 'Speedy', 19 November 1799–15 April 1800, 25 January 1800.
10   Robert Scott, Letters, 1800–1802, 16 August 1801.
11   HRA, series 1, vol. 3, pp. 264–65; Governor King to the Duke of Portland, 8 July 1801, HRA, series 1, vol. 3, p. 115.
12   Robert Scott, Letters, 1800–1802, 16 August 1801.
13   Flannery, *The Birth of Sydney*, p. 176.
14   Karskens, *The Rocks*, p. 19.
15   King to Portland, 10 March 1801, *Historical Records of New South Wales* (HRNSW), vol. 4, pp. 320, 404, 929.
16   Gapps, *The Sydney Wars*, p. 50.
17   Gapps, p. 142.
18   Irish, *Hidden in Plain View*, ch. 1.
19   Ralston, *Grass Huts and Warehouses*, p. 11.
20   Hainsworth, 'Lord, Simeon (1771–1840)', http://adb.anu.edu.au/biography/lord-simeon-2371/text3115
21   Melville, *Moby Dick*, p. 59.
22   Ralston, pp. 10, 11.
23   Flannery, p. 179.
24   Karskens, '"This spirit of emigration"', p. 12.
25   Webster, *Reminiscences of an Old Settler in Australia and New Zealand*, p. 56.
26   Hirst, *Freedom on the Fatal Shore*, p. 33.
27   Hirst, p. 29.
28   Flannery, p. 180.
29   Flannery, p. 162.
30   Australian Historical Population Statistics, www.abs.gov.au/AUSSTATS/abs@.nsf/DetailsPage/3105.0.65.0012006?OpenDocument

31 Robinson, p. 249.
32 For more of this argument see, for example, Oxley, *Convict Maids*, pp. 226–31.
33 Flannery, p. 163.
34 Oxley, p. 62.
35 Karskens, *The Colony*, p. 327.
36 Daniels, *Convict Women*, p. 89.
37 Daniels, p. 98.
38 Robinson, pp. 248–55.
39 Karskens, *The Colony*, p. 329.
40 King to Portland, 1 March 1802, HRA, series 1, vol. 3, p. 424.
41 Samuel Marsden essays concerning New South Wales, 1807–18--.
42 Samuel Marsden essays concerning New South Wales, 1807–18--.
43 Samuel Marsden essays concerning New South Wales, 1807–18--.
44 Robinson, p. 252; HRNSW, vol. 6, pp. 150–51.
45 Bigge, *Report on State of the Colony of New South Wales*, http://gutenberg.net.au/ebooks13/1300181h.html
46 *Sydney Gazette*, 20 July 1806, p. 1.
47 Karskens, *The Colony*, p. 316.
48 Damousi, p. 35.
49 Collins, *An Account of the English Colony of New South Wales*, vol. II, http://gutenberg.net.au/ebooks/e00011.html
50 Re the term 'grammar of difference', see Hall, 'Culture and Identity in Imperial Britain', pp. 203–4.
51 Damousi, p. 39.
52 HRNSW, vol. 6, p. 151.
53 Bigge, *Report on State of the Colony of New South Wales*, http://gutenberg.net.au/ebooks13/1300181h.html
54 De Vera, *An Australian Woman's Diary 1985*, n.p.
55 Cameron, 'Factory Above the Gaol', https://dictionaryofsydney.org/entry/factory_above_the_gaol
56 Oxley, p. 193.
57 Cameron, 'Parramatta Female Factory', https://dictionaryofsydney.org/entry/parramatta_female_factory; Oxley, p. 193.
58 Daniels, pp. 170–71.

The Pirate

1 Ballara, 'Te Pahi', https://teara.govt.nz/en/biographies/1t53/te-pahi
2 Belich, *Making Peoples*, p. 141.
3 Druett, 'Of Ships, and Seals, and Savage Coasts', p. 133. Stewart was brought back to Sydney on board the *Star* in June 1806. *Sydney Gazette*, 22 June 1806, p. 4.
4 *Sydney Gazette*, 20 July 1806, p. 1.
5 Vennell, *The Brown Frontier*, p. 19.
6 *Sydney Morning Herald*, 26 October 1937, p. 21.
7 Snowden, 'Lord, Maria (1780–1859)', https://adb.anu.edu.au/biography/lord-maria-13052/text23601. See also Daniels, *Convict Women*, ch. 1, p. 76.
8 Hirst, *Freedom on the Fatal Shore*, p. 100.
9 Daniels, p. 76.

10   Boyce, *Van Diemen's Land*, p. 109.
11   Daniels, p. 74.
12   Christopher, *A Merciless Place*, p. 48.
13   Criminal Registers Middlesex, 1796–1797.
14   Petition of J. W. Lancashire to Governor Hunter, 2 April 1799, HRA, series 1, vol. 2, p. 320.
15   'John William Lancashire', www.daao.org.au/bio/john-william-lancashire/biography
16   *Sydney Gazette*, 12 January 1806, p. 1.
17   'John William Lancashire', www.daao.org.au/bio/john-william-lancashire/biography
18   The *Tellicherry* subsequently wrecked off the coast of New Guinea. The crew all survived, and made for Manila, before going to Canton and then Calcutta, the ship's original destination. HRA, series 1, vol. 6, note 30, p. 712.
19   Journal of Richard Atkins, 1791–1810, p. 131. See also 'Reliance passenger list' for confirmation that Hagerty was on board.
20   List of persons who have obtained Lord Hobart's permission to proceed as Settlers to New South Wales, HRA, series 1, vol. 4, p. 451.
21   Atkinson, 'Richard Atkins: The Women's Judge', pp. 135, 140.
22   *Sydney Gazette*, 20 July 1806, p. 1.
23   Linebaugh and Rediker, *The Many-Headed Hydra*, p. 151; Melville, *Moby Dick*, p. 186.
24   *Sydney Gazette*, 13 July 1806, p. 4.
25   Druett, p. 134; *Sydney Gazette*, 6 April 1806, p. 2.
26   Governor King to Viscount Castlereagh, 27 July 1806, HRA, series 1, vol. 5, p. 753.
27   Linebaugh and Rediker, pp. 162–67.
28   Governor King to Sir Evan Nepean, 20 December 1804, HRA, series 1, vol. 5, pp. 238–39.
29   Christopher, '"Ten Thousand Times Worse Than the Convicts"', p. 35.
30   Haines and West, 'Crew Cultures in the Tasman World', p. 186.
31   Christopher, '"Ten Thousand Times Worse Than the Convicts"', pp. 41–42.
32   Maxwell-Stewart, '"Those Lads Contrived a Plan"', p. 191.
33   Karskens, '"This Spirit of Emigration"', p. 7.
34   Karskens, '"This Spirit of Emigration"', p. 15.
35   Karskens, '"This Spirit of Emigration"', p. 11.
36   Karskens, '"This Spirit of Emigration"', p. 6.
37   Maxwell-Stewart, p. 193.
38   Karskens, '"This Spirit of Emigration"', p. 13.
39   Becke, 'An Old Colonial Mutiny', *Ridan the Devil and Other Stories*. This story was first published in the *Evening News* (Sydney), 23 November 1895, p. 3.
40   Day, *Louis Becke*, p. 71.
41   *Evening News*, 23 November 1895, p. 3.
42   *Sydney Morning Herald*, 26 October 1937, p. 21. I talked about Becke's story of Badger in the *Evening News* and the later story in the *Sydney Morning Herald* in a Radio New Zealand interview in March 2018. See 'Pirate Mystery: The story of Charlotte Badger', www.rnz.co.nz/audio/player?audio_id=2018634264. The same point was made in June 2019 in Hardie, 'Was Charlotte Badger a Colonial Renegade?'

43   Ormsby, 'Badger, Charlotte', https://teara.govt.nz/en/biographies/1b1/badger-charlotte
44   Jeffrey, *A Century of Our Sea Story*, p. 297, https://archive.org/stream/acenturyourseas00jeffgoog/acenturyourseas00jeffgoog_djvu.txt
45   Belich, p. 132.
46   Brookes, *A History of New Zealand Women*, p. 2. Brookes makes specific reference to the Dictionary and the *Sydney Morning Herald* article.
47   Joe Cannon, quoted in Peat, *The Tasman*, p. 15.

The Beach Crosser

1   This study follows the findings of Deidre Brown, who identifies Wairoa Bay as Te Pahi's base. Brown argues, 'Accounts by early European visitors often confuse the name of the Wairoa Bay settlement with its neighbour, Te Puna, in Rangihoua Bay.' See Brown, 'Te Pahi's Whare: The first European house in New Zealand'. See also 'Appendix: Background Information for Rangihoua', www.nrc.govt.nz/media/nmwe4vxs/appendixbackgroundinformationforrangihouahistoricheritagearea.pdf. In addition, the painting reproduced in this book called *Tepoanah* resembles Wairoa Bay in the geography it depicts.
2   Neither Robert McNab nor Harry Morton, in their respective studies of visiting whalers, give any indication of Bunker's success in finding whales. McNab, *From Tasman to Marsden*; Morton, *The Whale's Wake*.
3   *Sydney Gazette*, 10 July 1803, p. 4.
4   Governor King to Earl Camden, 30 April 1805, Robert McNab, ed., *Historical Records of New Zealand* (HRNZ), vol. 1, p. 254.
5   *Sydney Gazette*, 5 June 1803, p. 4.
6   'On reaching Australia, Teina stayed with the Governor, Philip Gidley King. . . . Teina and another Maori, Maki, remained aboard the *Alexander* for the next three years, visiting Tahiti, Brazil, St Helena and eventually England, where Teina and two Tahitians subsequently died.' Cawthorn, *Maori, Whales and "Whaling"*, p. 4.
7   Anne Salmond, *Between Worlds*, p. 329.
8   King Papers, 2 January 1806, HRNZ, vol. 1, pp. 265–66.
9   Linebaugh and Rediker, *The Many-Headed Hydra*, p. 162.
10   Vennell, *The Brown Frontier*, p. 22; Salmond, p. 360.
11   *Evening News*, 23 November 1895, p. 3.
12   Dening, *Beach Crossings*.
13   Savage, *Some Account of New Zealand*, pp. 91–92, www.enzb.auckland.ac.nz/document/?wid=71
14   The Logbooks of the Lady Nelson, 12 June 1804, www.gutenberg.org/files/7509/7509-h/7509-h.htm
15   Salmond, p. 358.
16   Dening, *Beach Crossings*, p. 334.
17   Dening, *The Marquesan Journal of Edward Robarts*, p. 184.
18   George Bruce, 1778?–1819: Life of a Greenwich pensioner.
19   Salmond, pp. 289–94.
20   Papers of Sir Joseph Banks, 1745–1923; Salmond, p. 360.
21   Petrie, *Outcasts of the Gods?*, pp. 285–86. For the suggestion that Badger was held captive see also O'Malley, *The Meeting Place*, p. 161. O'Malley argues

that it 'may have been in response to the kidnapping and capture of a group of
Ngāpuhi women taken south by the remaining members of the vessel's crew'.

22   Petrie, p. 93.
23   Belich, *Making Peoples*, p. 133; O'Malley, *The Meeting Place*, p. 161; Brookes,
      A History of New Zealand Women, p. 20. See also Bentley, *Pakeha Slaves, Maori
      Masters*, pp. 237–38, where the author claimed that 'Charlotte Badger lived
      some nine years with a "lesser" Ngapuhi chief at the Bay of Islands'.
24   Evidence Given Before Commissioner Bigge by Ensign McCrae, HRNZ,
      vol. 1, p. 542.
25   Ralston, *Grass Huts and Warehouses*, p. 24.
26   *Sydney Gazette*, 12 April 1807, p. 1.
27   Bentley, p. 51.
28   *Sydney Gazette*, 12 April 1807, p. 2.
29   *Sydney Gazette*, 22 June 1806, p. 4.
30   *Sydney Gazette*, 24 August 1806, p. 3; 7 December 1806, p. 1.
31   *Sydney Gazette*, 12 April 1807, p. 1.
32   *Sydney Gazette*, 12 April 1807, p. 1.
33   *Sydney Gazette*, 8 February 1806, p. 2; 12 April 1807, p. 1.
34   List of persons who take passage in His Majesty's Ship Porpoise . . . to be landed
      at Port Jackson. I was alerted to Badger's passage on board the *Indispensible* by
      David Povey. David Povey, email to author, 31 January 2019.
35   Sherrin and Wallace, *Early History of New Zealand*, p. 134; McNab, *From Tasman
      to Marsden*, pp. 110–12; Jack Lee, *'I Have Named it the Bay of Islands . . .'*, p. 43.
36   Ormsby, 'Badger, Charlotte', https://teara.govt.nz/en/biographies/1b1/
      badger-charlotte
37   Salmond, p. 361; O'Malley, *The Meeting Place*, p. 161.
38   *Evening News*, 23 November 1895, p. 3.
39   *Sydney Morning Herald*, 26 October 1937, p. 21.
40   Stackpole, *The Sea-Hunters*, p. 399.
41   Morton, p. 89.
42   Morton, pp. 95, 125.
43   Becke, 'The Adventure of Elizabeth Morey of New York', in *The Tapu of
      Banderah and Other Stories*. For a historical discussion of Morey's story see
      Hughes, 'Elizabeth Morey: Castaway in Tonga, 1802–1804'.
44   'Pickled Fish and Salted Provisions: Oil and Bone: Salem's Whaling Industry',
      http://npshistory.com/publications/sama/newsletter/v11n2.pdf
45   Elder, *The Letters and Journals of Samuel Marsden 1865–1838*, p. 108.
46   Nicholas, *Narrative of a Voyage to New Zealand*, pp. 417–18.
47   McNab, *From Tasman to Marsden*, p. 112.
48   *Sydney Gazette*, 12 April 1807, p. 1.
49   *Sydney Gazette*, 29 May 1808, p. 1.
50   Vennell, p. 27.
51   Pereira Salas, 'Las primeras relaciones entre Chile y Australia', pp. 5–36.
52   Duffield, 'Cutting Out and Taking Liberties', pp. 197–227.

The Army Wife

1   List of persons who take passage in His Majesty's Ship Porpoise . . . to be landed
      at Port Jackson.

2   Viscount Palmerston to Governor Macquarie, 1 March 1810, HRA, series 1, vol. 7, p. 210.

3   I talked about Badger's return to New South Wales and marriage to Humphries in a Radio New Zealand interview in March 2018. See 'Pirate Mystery: The story of Charlotte Badger', www.rnz.co.nz/audio/player?audio_id=2018634264

4   'Church Hill', PocketOz Pocket Guide to Sydney, www.visitsydneyaustralia.com.au/church-hill.html

5   Mutch Index of Births, Deaths and Marriages.

6   Buckley, 'The Destruction of the British Army in the West Indies 1793–1815', p. 79.

7   Thomas Humphries, Royal Hospital Chelsea: Soldiers Service Documents.

8   Hurl-Eamon, *Marriage and the British Army in the Long Eighteenth Century*.

9   Sargent, 'The British Garrison in Australia', p. 44.

10   Hurl-Eamon, p. 116.

11   Angers, 'Marrying a Redcoat', p. 46.

12   Macquarie to Lord Bathurst, 31 July 1813, HRA, series 1, vol. 8, p. 4.

13   Biographical Database of Australia, 'Charlotte Humphries'.

14   'Veteran soldiers in the British Army against Napoleon', www.bbc.co.uk/radio4/history/making_history/makhist10_prog2a.shtml

15   Lieutenant-Governor Paterson to Governor Bligh, 1 February 1807, HRA, series 1, vol. 6, p. 119.

16   Karskens, *The Colony*, p. 79.

17   A Soldier's Letter, 13 December 1794, HRNSW, vol. 2, p. 817.

18   Proclamation, 24 February 1810, HRNSW, vol. 7, p. 531.

19   Angers, p. 116. See also Trustram, *Women of the Regiment*, pp. 70–72; McKenna, '"My own character is thank God above suspicion"', pp. 485–89, 491.

20   McKenna, pp. 492–94.

21   Jones and Jenkins, *He Kōrero*, ch. 12.

22   Jones and Jenkins, ch. 12; Te Punga Somerville, 'Living on New Zealand Street', pp. 655–69.

23   Yarwood, 'Marsden, Samuel (1765–1838)', http://adb.anu.edu.au/biography/marsden-samuel-2433/text3237. See also Ashton, *At the Margin of Empire*, p. 22, for a discussion of the racial views of Europeans, particularly with regard to Aboriginal people.

24   Grimshaw and Evans, 'Colonial Women on Intercultural Frontiers', pp. 79–95; Vivers, 'Dealing with Difference', pp. 72–96.

25   Karskens, *The Colony*, p. 501.

26   *Sydney Gazette*, 31 December 1814, p. 2.

27   Irish, *Hidden in Plain View*, ch. 3.

28   Judge Barron Field, quoted in Irish, ch. 3.

29   King, quoted in Gapps, *The Sydney Wars*, p. 47.

30   Gapps, p. 130.

31   Gapps, p. 181.

32   Irish, ch. 3.

33   *Sydney Gazette*, 14 May 1814, p. 2.

34   Gapps, p. 230.

35   Colonial Secretary's Papers, 1788–1856, Main Series of Letters Received, https://ro.uow.edu.au/cgi/viewcontent.cgi?referer=https://www.google.com/&httpsredir=1&article=1496&context=asdpapers

36   Proclamation, 4 May 1816, HRA, series 1, vol. 9, pp. 141–45.
37   Proclamation, 1 November 1816, HRA, series 1, vol. 9, p. 365.
38   *Sydney Gazette*, 4 January 1817, p. 2.
39   For more on officers' wives see Angers, pp. 51–60, 106–113; McInnis, *Women of Empire*, ch. 4.
40   Bigge, *Report on State of the Colony of New South Wales*, http://gutenberg.net.au/ebooks13/1300181h.html
41   Bigge, *Report on State of the Colony of New South Wales*, http://gutenberg.net.au/ebooks13/1300181h.html
42   Bigge, *Report on State of the Colony of New South Wales*, http://gutenberg.net.au/ebooks13/1300181h.html
43   Macquarie to Bathurst, 16 May 1817, HRA, series 1, vol. 9, p. 405.
44   Sir Thomas Brisbane to Major-General Sir Herbert Taylor, 26 January 1822, HRA, series 1, vol. 10, p. 610.
45   *Sydney Gazette*, 2 October 1823, p. 2.
46   Gapps, p. 100.
47   Karskens, *The Colony*, p. 110.
48   Karskens, *The Colony*, pp. 127–28.
49   Thomas Humphries to Governor Darling, 9 December 1829.
50   Colonial Secretary to Thomas Humphries, 29 December 1829.
51   Clerk of the Peace: Registers of Criminal cases tried at country Quarter Sessions: Parramatta: 1839–1876, Windsor 1839–1843.

The Histories of Charlotte Badger

1   For further discussion of this see Nasaw, 'Introduction: Historians and Biography', p. 573.
2   Lipscomb, 'Gossiping with the Dead', www.historytoday.com/archive/making-history/gossiping-dead
3   Colley, *The Ordeal of Elizabeth Marsh*, p. xix.
4   Caine, *Biography and History*, p. 1.
5   Caine, p. 3.
6   Johnson, *A General History of the Pyrates*, p. 173, www.gutenberg.org/files/40580/40580-h/40580-h.htm
7   Linebaugh and Rediker, *The Many-Headed Hydra*, p. 167.
8   Damousi, *Depraved and Disorderly*, p. 19.
9   Montgomerie, 'New Women and Not-So-New Men', p. 52.
10 *Sydney Morning Herald*, 26 October 1937, p. 21; Brookes, *A History of New Zealand Women*, pp. 219–21.
11 Oxley, *Convict Maids*, p. 3; Robinson, *The Women of Botany Bay*, p. 8.
12 Dixson, *The Real Matilda*, p. 123; Lake, 'Women's and Gender History in Australia', p. 191.
13 Lake, p. 198.
14 Damousi, p. 3.
15 O'Connor, 'Review of Kay Daniels, *Convict Women*', p. 241.
16 Lake, p. 194.
17 Macdonald, Penfold and Williams, *The Book of New Zealand Women*, p. vii.
18 See, for example, Dalziel, 'The Colonial Helpmeet', pp. 112–23.

19   Macdonald, *A Woman of Good Character*, p. 175.
20   Ormsby, 'Badger, Charlotte', https://teara.govt.nz/en/biographies/1b1/badger-charlotte
21   Brookes, pp. 20–21.
22   *Evening News*, 23 November 1895, p. 3.
23   Hilliard, 'Stories of an Era Not Yet So Very Remote', pp. 28–39.
24   Vennell, *The Brown Frontier*.
25   Vennell, inner cover flyleaf.
26   See, for example, Judith Binney, *The Legacy of Guilt: A Life of Thomas Kendall*, Auckland University Press, Auckland, 1968; 2nd edn, Bridget Williams Books, Wellington, 2005; Alan Ward, *A Show of Justice: Racial 'Amalgamation' in Nineteenth Century New Zealand*, Auckland University Press, Auckland, 1973; M. P. K. Sorrenson, 'Maori and Pakeha', in W. H. Oliver and B. R. Williams (eds), *The Oxford History of New Zealand*, Oxford University Press, Oxford and Wellington, 1981, pp. 168–93.
27   O'Malley, *The Meeting Place*, p. 6. Greg Dening, whose work is used in chapter 4 (The Beach Crosser), is an example of this literature in a Pacific context. Dening, *Islands and Beaches*; Dening, *Beach Crossings*.
28   Salmond, *Between Worlds*, pp. 13, 14.
29   For other examples, see Atholl Anderson, *Race Against Time: The Early Maori-Pakeha Families and the Development of Mixed-race Population in Southern New Zealand*, Hocken Library, University of Otago, Dunedin, 1991; Angela Wanhalla, *In/visible Sight: The Mixed-Descent Families of Southern New Zealand*, Bridget Williams Books, Wellington, 2009; Binney, *Te Kerikeri 1770–1850*.
30   See, for example, Attwood and Foster, *Frontier Conflict*; Reynolds, *The Other Side of the Frontier*; Reynolds, *Forgotten War*; Gapps, *The Sydney Wars*; Irish, *Hidden in Plain View*.
31   This debate has been particularly contentious in Australia, which has experienced the so-called history wars. For an early background see McKenna, 'Different Perspectives on Black Armband History', www.aph.gov.au/About_Parliament/Parliamentary_Departments/Parliamentary_Library/pubs/rp/RP9798/98RP05
32   Ballantyne, *Orientalism and Race*, p. 14.
33   Ballantyne, *Orientalism and Race*, p. 1.
34   Rachel Standfield, 'Moving Across, Looking Beyond', p. 1.
35   See, for example, Ogborn, *Global Lives*, p. 10; Deacon, Russell and Woollacott, *Transnational Lives*.
36   Belich, *Making Peoples*, p. 132.
37   Snyder, 'What is Third-Wave Feminism?', pp. 179, 185.

Bibliography

Primary sources

Historical Records of Australia (HRA)
Historical Records of New South Wales (HRNSW)
Historical Records of New Zealand (HRNZ)

Alexander Turnbull Library, Wellington

George Bruce, 1778?–1819: Life of a Greenwich pensioner, MS-Copy-Micro-0538

Auckland Council Libraries

Baxter, Carol J. (ed.), General muster and land and stock muster of New South Wales, 1822, Sydney, 1988

Baxter, Carol J. (ed.), General muster list of New South Wales, 1823, 1824, 1825, Sydney, 1999

Baxter, Carol J. (ed.), Musters of New South Wales and Norfolk Island, 1805–1806, Sydney, 1989

Baxter, Carol J. (ed.), General musters of New South Wales, Norfolk Island and Van Diemen's Land, 1811, Sydney, 1987

The National Archives, London

Captain's Log, HMS Porpoise, Jan 1807–May 1808, ADM 51/4487

Correspondence and warrants, 7 June 1794–16 Aug 1796, HO 13/10

Correspondence and warrants, 13 Aug 1796–4 Sept 1797, HO 13/11

Correspondence and warrants, 7 June 1798–1 July 1800, HO 13/12

Criminal Registers Middlesex, 1796–1797, Newgate, HO 26/5

Journal of the Proceedings of His Majesty's Ship Reliance, between 1 Nov 1798 and 3 March 1800, ADM 51 1312

Newgate Prison Calendar, HO 77/3

Newgate Prison, London: lists of felons (prisoners) on the Master's Side, 1794 Jan–1801 July, PCOM 2/180

Newgate Prison, London: lists of felons (prisoners) on the Common Side, 1794 Jan–1797 Dec, PCOM 2/181

Oxford Circuit Assizes, Crown minute book, 1791 Summer–1799 Lent, ASSI 2/26

Reliance passenger list, ADM 36/13399

Sheriffs' Assizes Vouchers, 1795–1800, E389/250

Sheriffs' Cravings, 1794–1799, T90/168

Thomas Humphries, Royal Hospital Chelsea: Soldiers Service Documents, WO 97/1141/98

Transportation register of convicts bound for New South Wales on the convict ship Earl Cornwallis, HO 11/1/275

Worcestershire: Worcester. Plan of the county gaol and bridewell, showing cells and other buildings and offices, adjacent premises with their occupiers and rents, MPE 1-1551

Worcester Castle: the site, and remains used as a gaol, CRES 39-3

National Library of Australia

Journal of Richard Atkins, 1791–1810, MS 4039

Papers of Sir Joseph Banks, 1745–1923, MS 9, Series 3, item 139-139d

Robert Scott, Letters, 1800–1802, MS 1898

New South Wales State Archives

Bench of Magistrates Index 1788–1820, reels 655 and 656

Catherine Hagarty, Absolute Pardon, Convicts Index 1791–1873, item 4/4486, reel 800

Clerk of the Peace: Registers of Criminal cases tried at country Quarter Sessions: Parramatta: 1839–1876, Windsor: 1839–1843, reel 2757

Colonial Secretary to Thomas Humphries, 29 December 1829, NRS 944: Individuals, Organisations etc re Land, item 4/3559, reel 2299

Colonial Secretary's Papers, 1788–1856, Main Series of Letters Received

Criminal Court Records Index 1788-1833, Appendix A: Schedule of prisoners tried, 1788–1815 – Court of Criminal Jurisdiction: Minutes of proceedings, 1788–1815, reel 2651

Criminal Court Records Index 1788–1833, Appendix D: Indictments, informations and related papers, 1796–1815 – Court of Criminal Jurisdiction: Informations, depositions and related papers, 1796–1824, reel 2392

List of persons who take passage in His Majesty's Ship Porpoise . . . to be landed at Port Jackson [4_1168A], COD429, Colonial Secretary's Letters

Thomas Humphries to Governor Darling, 9 December 1829, Colonial Secretary's Letters relating to Land 1826–56, item 2/7886, reel 1142

Parliamentary Archives, London

Petition of the Prisoners for Debt in the County Gaol of Worcester complaining of their Distress and Praying Relief, 28 April 1794, HL PO JO 10/7/989

State Library of New South Wales

Anna Josepha King journal of a voyage from England to Australia in the ship 'Speedy', 19 November 1799–15 April 1800, Mitchell Library

Invalid Company/Veterans Company NSW, reel PRO 417/11228, WO 12/11228; reel PRO 418, WO 12/11229; Mitchell Library

Mutch Index of Births, Deaths and Marriages

Samuel Marsden essays concerning New South Wales, 1807–18--, with list of females in the colony, 1806?, MLMSS 18, Mitchell Library

Worcestershire Archive and Archaeology Service

Benjamin Wright, Worcestershire Original Wills Part 2 1694–1857, reel 425

County of Worcester Quarter Sessions Order Books, Worcester County Archive, 118 BA 6 vol 6 (1791–1795)

County Gaol Visiting Magistrates Minutes, vol 1 1794–1821, series 122

Index of Apprentices Indentures

Parish Register St John the Baptist Bromsgrove, Baptisms and Burials 1774–1783

Worcester Court of Quarter Session, Session Papers 1750–1799

Newspapers

Berrows Worcester Journal

Bromsgrove Rousler

Evening News (Sydney)

Sydney Gazette

Sydney Morning Herald

Worcester Herald

Secondary sources

Articles & book chapters

Anderson, Clare, '"Multiple Border Crossings": Convicts and Other Persons Escaped from Botany Bay and residing in Calcutta', *Journal of Australian Colonial History*, vol. 3, no. 2, 2001, pp. 1–22

Atkinson, Alan, 'Richard Atkins: The Women's Judge', *Journal of Australian Colonial History*, vol. 1, no. 1, 1999, pp. 115–42

Baigent, Elizabeth, Charlotte Brewer and Vivienne Larminie, 'Gender in the Archive: Women in the *Oxford Dictionary of National Biography* and the *Oxford English Dictionary*', *Archives*, vol. 30, pp. 13–35, preprint version

Ballantyne, Tony, 'Maritime Connections and the Colonisation of New Zealand', in Frances Steel (ed.), *New Zealand and the Sea: Historical Perspectives*, Bridget Williams Books, Wellington, 2018, pp. 106–28

Binney, Judith, 'Tuki's Universe', *New Zealand Journal of History*, 38, 2 (2004), pp. 215–32

Bradley, J., 'The Colonel and the Slave Girls: Life Writing and the Logic of History in 1830s Sydney', *Journal of Social History*, vol. 42, no. 2, Winter 2011, pp. 416–35

Brown, Deidre, 'Te Pahi's Whare: The First European House in New Zealand', revision of paper originally presented and published at SAHANZ conference, University of Tasmania, 2012

Buckley, Roger N., 'The Destruction of the British Army in the West Indies 1793–1815: A Medical History', *Journal of the Society for Army Historical Research*, vol. 56, no. 226, 1978, pp. 79–82

Byrne, Paula J., 'Convict Women Reconsidered . . . and Reconsidered', *History Australia*, vol. 2, no. 1, 2004, pp. 13-1–13-3

Christopher, Emma, '"Ten Thousand Times Worse than the Convicts": Rebellious Sailors, Convict Transportation and the Struggle for Freedom, 1787–1800', *Journal of Australian Colonial History*, vol. 5, 2004, pp. 30–46

Dalziel, Raewyn, 'The Colonial Helpmeet: Women's Role and the Vote in Nineteenth-Century New Zealand', *New Zealand Journal of History*, 11, 2 (1977), pp. 112–23

Davis, Michael T., 'Bread Riots, Britain, 1795', *The International Encyclopedia of Revolution and Protest*, 20 April 2009, https://doi.org/10.1002/9781405198073.wbierp0243

Druett, Joan, 'Of Ships, and Seals, and Savage Coasts: Samuel Rodman Chace in the Southern Ocean, 1798–1821', *Journal of New Zealand Studies*, no. 2/3 (2004), pp. 129–48

Duffield, Ian, '"Haul Away the Anchor Girls": Charlotte Badger, Tall Stories and the Pirates of the "Bad Ship Venus"', *Journal of Australian Colonial History*, vol. 7, 2005, pp. 35–64

——, 'Cutting Out and Taking Liberties: Australia's Convict Pirates, 1790–1829', *International Review of Social History*, vol. 58, no. S21, 2013, pp. 197–227

Evans, Tanya, 'Secrets and Lies: The Radical Potential of Family History', *History Workshop Journal*, no. 71, Spring 2011, pp. 49–73

Frykman, Nklas, Clare Anderson, Lex Heerma van Voss and Marcus Rediker, 'Mutiny and Maritime Radicalism in the Age of Revolution: An Introduction', *International Review of Social History*, vol. 58, no. S21, 2013, pp. 1–14

Garton, Stephen, 'The Convict Origins Debate: Historians and the Problem of the "Criminal Class"', *Australian & New Zealand Journal of Criminology*, no. 24, 1991, pp. 66–82

Griffin, Emma, 'Hunger and Living Standards during the British Industrial Revolution', *Past & Present*, vol. 239, issue 1, May 2018, pp. 71–111

Grimshaw, Patricia and Julie Evans, 'Colonial Women on Intercultural Frontiers: Rosa Campbell Praed, Mary Bundock and Katie Langloh Parker', *Australian Historical Studies*, vol. 27, no. 106, 1996, pp. 79–95

Haines, David and Jonathan West, 'Crew Cultures in the Tasman World', in Frances Steel (ed.), *New Zealand and the Sea: Historical Perspectives*, Bridget Williams Books, Wellington, 2018, pp. 181–200

Hall, Catherine, 'Culture and Identity in Imperial Britain', in Sarah Stockwell (ed.), *The British Empire: Themes and Perspectives*, Blackwell Publishing, Oxford, 2008, pp. 199–221

Hardie, Elsbeth, 'Was Charlotte Badger a Colonial Renegade?', *Journal of New Zealand Studies*, no. NS28, 2019, https://doi.org/10.26686/jnzs.v0iNS28.5422

Hilliard, Chris, 'Stories of an Era Not Yet So Very Remote: James Cowan in and out of New Zealand History', *Journal of New Zealand Studies*, no. 19, 2015, pp. 28–39

Hughes, Shirley, 'Elizabeth Morey: Castaway in Tonga, 1802–1804', *Journal of Pacific History*, vol. 34, no. 1, June 1999, pp. 45–58

Junod, Tom, 'The Falling Man: An Unforgettable Story', *Esquire*, 9 September 2016

Karskens, Grace, '"This Spirit of Emigration": The Nature and Meanings of Escape in Early New South Wales', *Journal of Australian Colonial History*, vol. 7, 2005, pp. 1–34

King, Peter and Richard Ward, 'Rethinking the Bloody Code in Eighteenth-Century Britain: Capital Punishment at the Centre and on the Periphery', *Past & Present*, vol. 228, issue 1, August 2015, pp. 159–205

Lake, Marilyn, 'Women's and Gender History in Australia: A Transformative Practice', *Journal of Women's History*, vol. 25, no. 4, 2013, pp. 190–211

Lepore, J., 'Historians Who Love Too Much: Reflections on Microhistory and Biography', *Journal of American History*, vol. 88, no. 1, 2001, pp. 129–44

Lester, Alan, 'Imperial Circuits and Networks: Geographies of the British Empire', *History Compass*, vol. 4, issue 1, 2006, pp. 124–41

McKenna, Katherine M. J., '"My Own Character is Thank God Above Suspicion": Soldiers' Wives with The Royal Canadian Rifle Regiment and Social Values in Mid-Nineteenth-Century British North America', *Social History*, vol. XLIX, no. 100, November 2016, pp. 475–502

Maxwell-Stewart, Hamish, '"Those Lads Contrived a Plan": Attempts at Mutiny on Australia-Bound Convict Vessels', *International Review of Social History*, vol. 58, no. S21, 2013, pp. 177–96

Middleton, Angela, 'Maori and European Landscapes at Te Puna, Bay of Islands, New Zealand, 1805–1850', *Archaeology Oceania*, vol. 38, no. 2, 2003, pp. 110–24

Montgomerie, Deborah, 'New Women and Not-So-New Men: Discussions about Marriage in New Zealand, 1890–1914', *New Zealand Journal of History*, 51, 1 (2017), pp. 36–64

Nasaw, David, 'Introduction: Historians and Biography', *American Historical Review*, vol. 114, no. 3, 2009, pp. 573–78

O'Connor, Tamsin, 'Review of Kay Daniels, *Convict Women*', *Labour History*, no. 79, November 2000, pp. 240–42

Pereira Salas, Eugenio, 'Las Primeras Relaciones Entre Chile y Australia', *Academia Chilena de la Historia*, 1 January 1955, pp. 5–36

Picton Phillipps, Tina, 'Family Matters: Bastards, Orphans and Baptisms – New South Wales, 1810–1825', *Journal of the Royal Australian Historical Society*, vol. 90, no. 2, December 2004, pp. 122–35

Quinlan, Michael and Hamish Maxwell Stewart, 'Female Convict Labour and Absconding Rates in Colonial Australia', *Tasmanian Historical Studies*, vol. 22, 2017, pp. 19–36

Sargent, Clem, 'The British Garrison in Australia: Conditions of Service – Wives and Children', *Sabretache*, vol. XLIII, December 2002, pp. 15–21

Snyder, R. Claire, 'What Is Third-Wave Feminism? A New Directions Essay', *Signs*, vol. 34, no. 1, Autumn 2008, pp. 175–96

Standfield, Rachel, 'Moving Across, Looking Beyond', in Rachel Standfield (ed.), *Indigenous Mobilities: Across and Beyond the Antipodes*, ANU Press and Aboriginal History Inc., Canberra, 2018, pp. 1–34

——, 'Mobility, Reciprocal Relationships and Early British Encounters in the North of New Zealand', in Rachel Standfield (ed.), *Indigenous Mobilities: Across and Beyond the Antipodes*, ANU Press and Aboriginal History Inc., Canberra, 2018, pp. 57–78

Stern, Walter M., 'The Bread Crisis in Britain, 1795–96', *Economica*, New Series, vol. 31, no. 122, May 1964, pp. 171–72

Te Punga Somerville, Alice, 'Living on New Zealand Street: Maori Presence in Parramatta', *Ethnohistory*, vol. 61, no. 4, 2014, pp. 655–69

Vivers, Meg, 'Dealing with Difference: Evidence of European Women in Early Contact History', *Journal of Australian Colonial History*, vol. 4, no. 2, 2002, pp. 72–96

Wolpert, S., 'Biography as History: A Personal Reflection', *Journal of Interdisciplinary History*, vol. 40, no. 3, 2010, pp. 399–412

Wright, Christine, 'Military Settlers: The Men of the Royal Veteran Companies and Royal Staff Corps (1825)', *Journal of the Royal Australian Historical Society*, vol. 95, no. 2, November 2009, pp. 158–75

Books

Ashton, Jennifer, *At the Margin of Empire: John Webster and Hokianga 1841–1900*, Auckland University Press, Auckland, 2015

Attwood, B. and S. G. Foster, *Frontier Conflict: The Australian Experience*, National Museum of Australia, Canberra, 2003

Badger, Angela, *Charlotte Badger: Buccaneer*, Indra Publishing, Briar Hill, Victoria, 2002

Ballantyne, Tony, *Orientalism and Race: Aryanism in the British Empire*, Houndmills, Palgrave Macmillan, Basingstoke, Hampshire; New York, 2002

——, *Webs of Empire: Locating New Zealand's Colonial Past*, Bridget Williams Books, Wellington, 2012

Bateson, Charles, *The Convict Ships 1787–1868*, A. H. & A. W. Reed, Sydney, 1974

Becke, Louis, *Rídan the Devil and Other Stories*, T. Fisher Unwin, London, 1899

——, *The Tapu of Banderah and Other Stories*, C. A. Pearson, London, 1901

Belich, James, *Making Peoples: A History of the New Zealanders from Polynesian Settlement to the End of the Nineteenth Century*, Allen Lane, Auckland, 1996

Bentley, Trevor, *Pakeha Maori: The Extraordinary Story of the Europeans who Lived as Maori in Early New Zealand*, Penguin, Auckland, 1999

——, *Pakeha Slaves, Maori Masters: The Forgotten Story of New Zealand's White Slaves*, New Holland Publishers, Auckland, 2019

Binney, J. (ed.), *Te Kerikeri 1770–1850: The Meeting Pool*, Bridget Williams Books, Wellington, 2007

Boyce, James, *Van Diemen's Land*, Black Inc., Melbourne, 2008

Brookes, Barbara, *A History of New Zealand Women*, Bridget Williams Books, Wellington, 2016

Brooks, J. F., C. R. N. DeCorse and J. Walton, *Small Worlds: Method, Meaning & Narrative in Microhistory*, School for Advanced Research Press, Santa Fe, 2008

Caine, Barbara, *Biography and History*, Palgrave Macmillan, Basingstoke, 2010

Calder, A., J. Lamb and B. Orr (eds), *Voyages and Beaches: Pacific Encounters 1769–1840*, University of Hawai'i Press, Honolulu, 1999

Cawthorn, M. W., *Maori, Whales and "Whaling": An Ongoing Relationship*, Department of Conservation, Wellington, 2000

Christopher, Emma, *A Merciless Place: The Lost Story of Britain's Convict Disaster in Africa and How it Led to the Settlement of Australia*, Allen & Unwin, Crows Nest, NSW, 2010

Colley, Linda, *The Ordeal of Elizabeth Marsh: A Woman in World History*, Harper Press, New York, 2007

Cox, David J., *Crime in England 1688–1815*, Routledge, London and New York, 2015

Cunningham, Peter, *Two Years in New South Wales: A Series of Letters Comprising Sketches of the Actual State of Society in that Colony; of Its Peculiar Advantages to Emigrants; of Its Topography, Natural History*, vol. 1, Henry Colborn, London, 1827

Damousi, Joy, *Depraved and Disorderly: Female Convicts, Sexuality and Gender in Colonial Australia*, Cambridge University Press, Cambridge, 1997

Daniels, Kay, *Convict Women*, Allen & Unwin, St Leonards, NSW, 1998

Darwin, John, *Unfinished Empire: The Global Expansion of Britain*, Bloomsbury Press, London, 2012

Day, A. Grove, *Louis Becke*, Twayne Publishers, New York, 1966

Deacon, D., P. Russell and A. Woollacott, *Transnational Lives: Biographies in Global Modernity*, Palgrave Macmillan, Basingstoke, 2010

Dening, Greg (ed.), *The Marquesan Journal of Edward Robarts*, 1797–1824, ANU Press, Canberra, 1974

——, *Islands and Beaches: Discourse on a Silent Land: Marquesas 1774–1880*, The Dorsey Press, Chicago, 1980

—— *Beach Crossings: Voyaging Across Times, Cultures, and Self*, The Miegunyah Press, Carlton, Victoria, 2004

De Vera, M., *An Australian Woman's Diary 1985*, Hale & Iremonger, Sydney, 1984

Dixson, Miriam, *The Real Matilda: Woman and Identity in Australia 1788 to the Present*, 3rd edn, Penguin, Ringwood, Victoria, 1994

Elder, J. (ed.), *The Letters and Journals of Samuel Marsden 1865–1838*, Coulls Somerville Wilkie, Ltd and A. H. Reed, Dunedin, 1932

Emsley, Clive, *Crime and Society in England, 1750–1900*, 4th edn, Routledge, London and New York, 2010

Flannery, Tim (ed.), *The Birth of Sydney*, Text Publishing, Melbourne, 1999

Fox, Karen (ed.), *'True Biographies of Nations?': The Cultural Journeys of Dictionaries of National Biography*, ANU Press, Acton, ACT, 2019

Gapps, Stephen, *The Sydney Wars: Conflict in the Early Colony, 1788–1817*, NewSouth Publishing, Sydney, 2018

Gilje, Paul A., *Liberty on the Waterfront: American Maritime Culture in the Age of Revolution*, University of Pennsylvania Press, Philadelphia, 2004

Grayland, Eugene, *Coasts of Treachery*, A. H. & A. W. Reed, Wellington & Auckland, 1963

Green, Valentine, *The History and Antiquities of the City and Suburbs of Worcester*, vol. II, W. Bulmer & Co., London, 1796

Grenville, Kate, *The Secret River*, Text Publishing, Melbourne, 2005

——, *Searching for the Secret River*, Text Publishing, Melbourne, 2006

Griffin, Emma, *Liberty's Dawn: A People's History of the Industrial Revolution*, Yale University Press, New Haven & London, 2013

Grimshaw, P. and R. McGregor (eds), *Collisions of Cultures and Identities: Settlers and Indigenous Peoples*, University of Melbourne, Melbourne, 2007

Gwilliam, Bill, *Old Worcester: People and Places*, Halfshire Books, Bromsgrove, 1993

Hancock, Tim, Peter King and Pamela Sharpe, *Chronicling Poverty: The Voices and Strategies of the English Poor, 1640–1840*, Palgrave Macmillan, Houndsmill, 1997

Hirst, John, *Freedom on the Fatal Shore: Australia's First Colony*, Black Inc., Melbourne, 2008

Hodes, Martha, *The Sea Captain's Wife: A True Story of Love, Race, and War in the Nineteenth Century*, W. W. Norton, New York, 2006

Hodgson, Antonia, *The Devil in the Marshalsea*, Hodder & Stoughton, London, 2014

Honeyman, Katrina, *Child Workers in England, 1780–1820*, Ashgate Publishing, Aldershot, 2007

Hughes, Robert, *The Fatal Shore: A History of the Transportation of Convicts to Australia, 1787–1868*, Vintage Books, London, 2003

Hurl-Eamon, Jennine, *Marriage and the British Army in the Long Eighteenth Century: 'The Girl I Left Behind Me'*, Oxford University Press, Oxford, 2014

Irish, Paul, *Hidden in Plain View: The Aboriginal People of Coastal Sydney*, NewSouth Publishing, Sydney, 2017

Jeffrey, Walter, *A Century of Our Sea Story*, John Murray, London, 1900

Johnson, Captain Charles, *A General History of the Pyrates*, C. Rivington, London, 1724

Jones, Alison and Kuni Jenkins, *He Kōrero – Words Between Us: First Māori–Pākehā Conversations on Paper*, Huia Publishers, Wellington, 2011

Karskens, Grace, *The Rocks: Life in Early Sydney*, Melbourne University Press, Melbourne, 1998

——, *The Colony: A History of Early Sydney*, Allen & Unwin, Crows Nest, NSW, 2010

King, Peter, *Crime, Justice, and Discretion in England, 1740–1820*, Oxford University Press, Oxford, 2000

——, *Crime and Law in England, 1750–1840: Remaking Justice at the Margins*, Cambridge University Press, Cambridge, 2006

Kirkby, Peter, *Child Labour in Britain, 1750–1870*, Palgrave Macmillan, Houndsmill, 2003

Lambert, D. and A. Lester (eds), *Colonial Lives Across the British Empire: Imperial Careering in the Long Nineteenth Century*, Cambridge University Press, Cambridge, 2006

Lee, Jack, *'I Have Named It the Bay of Islands . . .'*, Hodder & Stoughton, Auckland, 1983

Linebaugh, Peter and Marcus Rediker, *The Many-Headed Hydra: Sailors, Slaves, Commoners, and the Hidden History of the Revolutionary Atlantic*, Beacon Press, Boston, 2000

Macdonald, Charlotte, *A Woman of Good Character: Single Women as Immigrant Settlers in Nineteenth-century New Zealand*, Bridget Williams Books, Wellington, 1990

Macdonald, Charlotte, Merimeri Penfold and Bridget Williams (eds), *The Book of New Zealand Women: Ko Kui Ma Te Kaupapa*, Bridget Williams Books, Wellington, 1991

McInnis, Verity, *Women of Empire: Nineteenth-Century Army Officers' Wives in India and the U.S. West*, University of Oklahoma Press, Norman, Oklahoma, 2017

McNab, Robert, *From Tasman to Marsden: A History of Northern New Zealand from 1642 to 1818*, J. Wilkie & Co. Ltd, Dunedin, 1914

Mawer, Granville Allen, *Ahab's Trade: The Saga of South Seas Whaling*, Allen & Unwin, St Leonards, NSW, 2000

Mein-Smith, Philippa, Peter Hempenstall and Shaun Goldfinch, with Stuart McMillan and Rosemary Baird, *Remaking the Tasman World*, Canterbury University Press, Christchurch, 2008

Melville, Herman, *Moby Dick*, Longriver Press, Secaucus, New Jersey, 1976

Middleton, Angela, *Pēwhairangi: Bay of Islands Missions and Māori 1814 to 1845*, Otago University Press, Dunedin, 2014

Mokyr, Joel, *The Enlightened Economy: An Economic History of Britain, 1700–1850*, Yale University Press, New Haven and New York, 2009

Morton, Harry, *The Whale's Wake*, University of Otago Press, Dunedin, 1982

Mountfort, P., *The 1804 Voyages of Coromandel and Experiment Convict Transports: with Extracts from his Lordship's Despatches of 1802–03, Containing Directions & Prim Precise Advice on How to Manage the Colony of New South Wales*, Book House, Sydney, 2002

Neild, James, *State of the Prisons in England, Scotland, and Wales*, John Nichols and Son, London, 1812

Nicholas, J. L., *Narrative of a Voyage to New Zealand*, vol. 1, James Black & Son, London, 1817

Ogborn, Miles, *Global Lives: Britain and the World 1550–1800*, Cambridge University Press, Cambridge, 2008

O'Malley, Vincent, *The Meeting Place: Māori and Pākehā Encounters, 1642–1840*, Auckland University Press, Auckland, 2012

——, *Haerenga: Early Māori Journeys Across the Globe*, Bridget Williams Books, Wellington, 2015

Oxley, Deborah, *Convict Maids: The Forced Migration of Women to Australia*, Cambridge University Press, Cambridge, 1996

Palk, Deirdre, *Gender, Crime and Judicial Discretion, 1780–1830*, Boydell Press, Woodbridge, Suffolk, 2006

Parry, Lorae, *Vagabonds*, Victoria University Press, Wellington, 2002

Peat, Neville, *The Tasman: Biography of an Ocean*, Penguin, Auckland, 2010

Petrie, Hazel, *Outcasts of the Gods? The Struggle over Slavery in Māori New Zealand*, Auckland University Press, Auckland, 2015

Ralston, Caroline, *Grass Huts and Warehouses: Pacific Beach Communities of the Nineteenth Century*, University of Hawai'i Press, Honolulu, 1978

Reynolds, H., *The Other Side of the Frontier: Aboriginal Resistance to the European Invasion of Australia*, Penguin, Ringwood, Victoria, 1982

——, *Fate of a Free People*, 2nd edn, Penguin, Camberwell, Victoria, 2004

——, *Forgotten War*, NewSouth Publishing, Sydney, 2013

Robinson, Portia, *The Women of Botany Bay*, Penguin, Ringwood, Victoria, 1993

Ross, John O'Connell, *William Stewart: Sealing Captain, Trader and Speculator*, Roebuck, Canberra, 1987

Russell, L. (ed.), *Colonial Frontiers: Indigenous–European Encounters in Settler Societies*, Manchester University Press, Manchester; New York, 2001

Salmond, Anne, *Between Worlds: Early Exchanges Between Maori and Europeans 1773–1815*, Penguin, Auckland, 2018

Sharp, Andrew, *The World, the Flesh & the Devil: The Life and Opinions of Samuel Marsden in England and the Antipodes, 1765–1838*, Auckland University Press, Auckland, 2016

Sherrin, R. A. A. and J. H. Wallace, *Early History of New Zealand: From Earliest Times to 1840*, H. Brett, Auckland, 1890

Smith, Babette, *A Cargo of Women: Susannah Watson and the Convicts of the Princess Royal*, Allen & Unwin, Crows Nest, NSW, 2008

Stackpole, Edouard A., *The Sea-Hunters: The New England Whalemen During Two Centuries*, J. B. Lippincott Company, Philadelphia, New York, 1953

Stanley, Peter, *The Remote Garrison: The British Army in Australia 1788–1870*, Kangaroo Press, Kenthurst, NSW, 1986

Steel, Frances (ed.), *New Zealand and the Sea: Historical Perspectives*, Bridget Williams Books, Wellington, 2018

The Historic Environment of Bromsgrove Town Centre, Worcestershire: A Baseline Survey, Worcestershire County Council, Worcester, 2013

Thomas, Nicholas, *Islanders: The Pacific in the Age of Empire*, Yale University Press, New Haven, 2012

Trustram, Myna, *Women of the Regiment: Marriage and the Victorian Army*, Cambridge University Press, Cambridge, 1984

Vennell, C. W., *The Brown Frontier: New Zealand 1806–1877*, A. H. & A. W. Reed, Wellington, 1967

Wadsworth, James E., *Global Piracy: A Documentary History of Seaborne Banditry*, Bloomsbury Academic, London, 2019

Webster, John, *Reminiscences of an Old Settler in Australia and New Zealand*, Whitcombe & Tombs, Christchurch, 1908

White, Jerry, *London in the Eighteenth Century: A Great and Monstrous Thing*, The Bodley Head, London, 2012

Williams, Samantha, *Poverty, Gender and Life-cycle under the English Poor Law, 1760–1834*, Boydell & Brewer, Woodbridge, 2011

Williams Milcairns, S*., Native Strangers: Beachcombers, Renegades and Castaways in the South Seas*, Penguin, Auckland, 2006

Unpublished sources

Angers, Séverine, 'Marrying a Redcoat: Women's Experiences of Marriage in the British Garrison of Quebec City, 1763–1820', MA thesis, Queen's University, Ontario, Canada, 2021

Charlotte Badger Research File, Dictionary of New Zealand Biography, Ministry for Culture and Heritage

Reid, Kirsty M., 'Work, Sexuality and Resistance: The Convict Women of Van Diemen's Land, 1820–1839', PhD thesis, University of Edinburgh, Edinburgh, 1995

Online sources

'Appendix: Background Information for Rangihoua', NRC ID15, www.nrc.govt.nz/media/nmwe4vxs/appendixbackgroundinformationforrangihouahistoricheritagearea.pdf

Ballara, Angela, 'Te Pahi', Dictionary of New Zealand Biography, first published in 1990, Te Ara – the Encyclopedia of New Zealand, https://teara.govt.nz/en/biographies/1t53/te-pahi

Barrett, Emma, 'Gendered Justice? The Fate of Convicted Murderers at the Old Bailey, 1780–1880', The Digital Panopticon, https://blog.digitalpanopticon.org/gendered-justice-the-fate-of-convicted-murderers-at-the-old-bailey-1780-1880

Bigge, John Thomas, *Report on State of the Colony of New South Wales*, http://gutenberg.net.au/ebooks13/1300181h.html

Biographical Database of Australia, 'Charlotte Humphries', www.bda-online.org.au/mybda/search/biographical-report/30009008301?f=Charlotte&l=Humphries&ol=&i=3&s=&p=

Cameron, Michaela Ann, 'Parramatta Female Factory', Dictionary of Sydney, https://dictionaryofsydney.org/entry/parramatta_female_factory

——, 'The Factory Above the Gaol', Dictionary of Sydney, https://dictionaryofsydney.org/entry/factory_above_the_gaol

Collins, David, *An Account of the English Colony of New South Wales*, vol. II, http://gutenberg.net.au/ebooks/e00011.html

Dickens, Charles, *Sketches by Boz: Illustrative of Every-Day Life and Every-Day People*, www.gutenberg.org/files/882/882-h/882-h.htm

Digital Panopticon, www.digitalpanopticon.org

Hainsworth, D. R., 'Lord, Simeon (1771–1840)', Australian Dictionary of Biography, National Centre of Biography, Australian National University, first published in 1967, http://adb.anu.edu.au/biography/lord-simeon-2371/text3115

'John William Lancashire', Design & Art Australia Online, www.daao.org.au/bio/john-william-lancashire/biography/

Laird, *Topographical and Historical Description of the County of Worcester, c. 1814*, www.parishmouse.co.uk/worcestershire/bromsgrove-worcestershire-family-history-guide/

Lipscomb, Susannah, 'Gossiping with the Dead', *History Today*, vol. 69, no. 12, December 2019, www.historytoday.com/archive/making-history/gossiping-dead

The Logbooks of the Lady Nelson, 12 June 1804, www.gutenberg.org/files/7509/7509-h/7509-h.htm

McKenna, Mark, 'Different Perspectives on Black Armband History', Politics and Public Administration Group, 10 November 1997, www.aph.gov.au/About_Parliament/Parliamentary_Departments/Parliamentary_Library/pubs/rp/RP9798/98RP05

Mantel, Hilary, 'The Day is for the Living', Reith Lecture 1, 13 June 2017, http://downloads.bbc.co.uk/radio4/reith2017/reith_2017_hilary_mantel_lecture1.pdf

——, 'The Iron Maiden', Reith Lecture 2, 20 June 2017, http://downloads.bbc.co.uk/radio4/reith2017/reith_2017_hilary_mantel_lecture2.pdf

'Nail Making in Bromsgrove', http://bromsgrovenailmaking.wixsite.com/nail-making/untitled-c139r

Old Bailey Proceedings Online, Crimes Tried at the Old Bailey: Housebreaking, www.oldbaileyonline.org/static/Crimes.jsp#housebreaking

Old Bailey Proceedings Online, trial of William John Lancashire, April 1796 (t17960406-14), www.oldbaileyonline.org/browse.jsp?id=t17960406-14-defend168&div=t17960406-14

Ormsby, Mary Louise, 'Badger, Charlotte', Dictionary of New Zealand Biography, first published in 1990, Te Ara – the Encyclopedia of New Zealand, https://teara.govt.nz/en/biographies/1b1/badger-charlotte

'Pickled Fish and Salted Provisions: Oil and Bone: Salem's Whaling Industry', National Park Service, U.S. Department of the Interior, http://npshistory.com/publications/sama/newsletter/v11n2.pdf

'Pirate Mystery: The story of Charlotte Badger', Radio New Zealand, 19 March 2018, www.rnz.co.nz/audio/player?audio_id=2018634264

Reihana, Lisa, 'Nomads of the Sea', 2019, www.lisareihana.com/nomads-of-the-sea

Savage, John, *Some Account of New Zealand*, 1805, pp. 91–92, www.enzb.auckland.ac.nz/document/?wid=71

Snowden, Dianne, 'Lord, Maria (1780–1859)', Australian Dictionary of Biography, National Centre of Biography, Australian National University, https://adb.anu.edu.au/biography/lord-maria-13052/text23601

Thomas, David, 'The real Little Dorrit: Charles Dickens and the debtors' prison', National Archives Lecture, 28 November 2008, https://media.nationalarchives.gov.uk/index.php/the-real-little-dorrit-charles-dickens-and-the-debtors-prison

'Veteran Soldiers in the British Army Against Napoleon', BBC, www.bbc.co.uk/radio4/history/making_history/makhist10_prog2a.shtml

Yarwood, A. T., 'Marsden, Samuel (1765–1838)', Australian Dictionary of Biography, National Centre of Biography, Australian National University, first published 1967, http://adb.anu.edu.au/biography/marsden-samuel-2433/text3237

Acknowledgements

My quest to find Charlotte Badger started years ago, and in the time since I have accumulated debts that I can only repay with gratitude.

A New Zealand History Research Trust Fund grant from the Ministry for Culture and Heritage allowed me to travel to the United Kingdom, Sydney and Wellington to carry out research in 2016. On these trips, I was grateful for the assistance of archivists and librarians at the Worcestershire Archive in Worcester, National Archives in London, the Mitchell Library and the New South Wales State Archives in Sydney, and the Alexander Turnbull Library in Wellington. Simon Gough of the Parliamentary Archives in London was particularly helpful in rearranging a visit following a flood in the Palace of Westminster! Thanks also to Mike Sharpe from the Bromsgrove Society for sending me copies of the *Bromsgrove Rousler* once I was back home.

My thanks to David Povey for emailing me with information about Badger's trip back to Sydney on the *Indispensible*, which I was able to follow up at the NSW State Archives. This kind of tip-off makes a historian's job much easier, and I appreciate David's generosity.

Sam Elworthy has been a patient and encouraging publisher, and his team at AUP have been a pleasure to work with. Thanks to Sophia Broom for her efficient and friendly organisation, and to Katharina Bauer and Lauren Donald for their assistance in checking the text. Thanks also to Caren Wilton for her careful editing and Mike Wagg for proofreading, Glenys Daley for her indexing skills,

Xoë Hall for her original artwork, Carolyn Lewis for her design and Tim Nolan for his map-making.

I appreciated the helpful feedback from the anonymous reviewers of the draft manuscript. Thank you for the time you invested in the project.

Finally, thanks to all the family and friends who have listened to me think out loud over the past five years. Your interest has helped me get to the point where my version of Badger's story sees the light of day.

Index

Jennifer Ashton is an Auckland-based technical
writer and editor. In 2012 she completed a
PhD in history at the University of Auckland,
which was published by Auckland University Press
in 2015 as *At the Margin of Empire:
John Webster and Hokianga, 1841–1900.*